Acclaim for Felix Dennis

"He writes like a man obsessed… If Waugh were still alive, he would fall on Dennis's verse with a glad cry of recognition and approval."
— **John Walsh**, *The Independent*

"The unpredictable Felix Dennis, long known for publishing other things, now bursts forth as a 21st century Kipling. In the poor old mallarme'd and ezrapounded world of contemporary poetry, no poet is taken seriously if he rollicks and rolls with rhyme, meter, and melody and can be understood in fewer than four read-throughs. But the Kipling of Barrack-Room Ballads and The Recessional could not be denied, at long last, despite decades of fashionable vituperation. Kipling II, I predict, will be just as much trouble — which he enjoys making on stage as well as on page."
— **Tom Wolfe**, author

"I enjoy his poetry immensely…"
— **Mick Jagger**, singer, songwriter

"Shakespeare beware. Dennis the Menace is trying to bring poetry back to the masses."
— **Bob Simon**, *60 Minutes II*

"*A Glass Half Full* is funny, poignant and a breath of fresh air. I loved the whole thing."
— **Sarah Broadhurst**, *The Bookseller*

"At least one of these poems will be instantly anthologised."
— **Melvyn Bragg**, broadcaster and author

"…an engaging monster, filled with contradictions and reeking of sulphur."
— *The Times [of London]*

"I enjoyed *A Glass Half Full* more than I can possibly say, Brilliant!"
— **Helen Gurley Brown**, International Editor in Chief, *Cosmopolitan*

"*A Glass Half Full* blew me away. Dennis is a crouching tiger about to wreak mayhem amongst the bleating lambs of English poetry."
— **Mick Farren**, novelist and poet

"Dennis confronts issues ranging from the holocaust to Elvis with equal poetic and emotional skill. The verse sweeps from darkly poignant to hilariously funny."
— **John Severs**, *Ottakar's New Title Reviews*

"A knockout! Multi-layered, full of wisdom, compassion, humour and worldly insight."
— **Richard Neville**, author and broadcaster

"Serious, witty, thought provoking and moving. You may even cry! I loved it."
— **Dave Reynolds**, *Radio Warwick*

"This is the way poetry should be. The sort of book that can make poetry popular again."
— **Alex Frankel**, Review Index.co.uk (*Amazon.co.uk*)

"I don't think I have ever known such a sense of celebration and occasion in all of the years of our poetry programme… You feel he lived it so richly, so dangerously, to be 'so wise for our delight'."
— **Dr. Robert Woof**, CBE, Director of *The Wordsworth Trust*

"…the 'Did I Mention the Free Wine?' tour gets 11 out of 10 for flamboyance."
— *The Financial Times*

"He is almost a force of nature"
— **Jeff Fager**, 60 Minute II producer, *USA Today*

"I don't know which is better, hearing [him] read them aloud or reading the book itself."
— **Dotun Adebayo,** *BBC Radio London*

"The audience was simply blown away."
— **David Carey,** publisher, *The New Yorker* (quoted in *The Wall Street Journal*)

"*A Glass Half Full* is the poetry of real life… the power to raise a smile in one who never laughs; to wring tears from another who hasn't wept since kindergarten; and to bring a measure of consolation to the inconsolable."
— **Anita Lafford,** sculptor

"An unforgettable evening. To hear him perform [with the Royal Shakespeare Company] was an entertaining and awe-inspiring privilege."
— **Sandy Holt,** *The Stratford Herald*

"…a mixture of laddish good humour and puppyish impatience… avuncular with a hint of malice…"
— **Michael Pilgrim,** *Evening Standard*

"A complex and controversial performance… Many people were deeply moved by the humanity of his verse and by the range of his experience [in these] haunting poems."
— **Tom Wujec,** TED Conference, Monterey

"Exhilarating… great performance art."
— **James Daly,** *Red Herring.com*

"He is far prouder of being a best-selling poet than his starring role in the Rich List."
— **Philip Beresford,** editor *The Sunday Times Rich List*

"Dennis is on a crusade to challenge the obscurity of modern verse."
— **Matthew Rose,** *The Wall Street Journal*

"Those of you who missed Felix Dennis at his UK-wide tour appearances should weep. By the fourth poem he had the audience drinking out of his hand."
— **Don Barnard,** *Reviews Gate.com*

"Picture his voice as a mixture of Carl Sandburg and Winston Churchill."
— *Media Industry Newsletter*

"You can easily picture him with a shank of lamb in one hand and a goblet of mead in the other. [He] succeeds because he takes a shameless, impish delight in all forms of human desire."
— **Simon Dumenco,** *Folio*

"One can recreate the visual image so clearly — hearing, sense of touch, sense of smell — they are so evocative in his poetry. It's enthralling, really."
— **Isobel Yule,** consultant, *National Library for the Blind*

"He's a joy to have as a British person."
— **Chris Hughes,** Publishing Director, *Good Housekeeping*

"A fantastic collection! Rich, sumptuous and beautifully threaded."
— **Jon Snow,** *Channel 4* broadcaster

"*A Glass Half Full* by Felix Dennis is a wonderful read. His poems have depth and freshness of voice. He writes for himself and I want to listen. His thoughts come alive without fear and without a care in the world for what anyone thinks. He writes of love, sex, wine and life with an energy I haven't seen in many years. I read his poems with the same excitement that I read Richard Brautigan in college many years ago."
— **Mark J Spencer,** *Amazon.com*

LONE WOLF

Felix Dennis

LONE WOLF

Illustrations by Bill Sanderson

HUTCHINSON
LONDON

First Printed in 2004 by Hutchinson

The Random House Group Ltd
20 Vauxhall Bridge Road, SW1V 2SA

Random House Australia (Pty) Ltd
20 Alfred Street, Milsons Point, Sydney
New South Wales, Australia

Random House New Zealand Ltd
18 Poland Street, Glenfield,
Auckland, New Zealand

Random House South Africa (Pty) Ltd
Endulini, 5A Jubilee Road, Parktown 2193, South Africa

A CIP catalogue record for this book is available from the British Library

The Random House Group Limited Reg. No. 954009
www.randomhouse.co.uk

ISBN 0-09-180035-8

Papers used by Random House are natural, recyclable
products made from wood grown in sustainable forests. The
manufacturing processes conform to the environmental
regulations of the country of origin.

Set in Adobe Electra
Printed and bound in Great Britain by
Butler & Tanner Ltd, Frome and London

Cover and book design by Mike Dunn

For more information, tour dates and
commentary go to **www.felixdennis.com**

To my brother, Julian:
a steady man in an unsteady world

And to 'Abdul' Rowe,
my old English teacher and the first
man to tell me I could write

"I built myself a house of glass:
It took me years to make it:
And I was proud. But now, alas!
Would God someone would break it."
— Edward Thomas

Contents

Preface

'Slower!' they tell me, 'savour your voices,
Write only when muses refuse to forbear;
The seat of the pants on the seat of the chair
Will lead you to error, to fret and to rave.'
But starting past fifty has left me few choices—
And little is written by those in their grave.

A YEAR AND TWO MONTHS AGO I wrote most of what follows within the over-sized quotation marks. Rather than compose a new Preface I offer the thoughts of a velvet night in my garden-by-the-sea in Mustique, while the moon hung upside down on her back, the tree-frogs whistled in choirs and phantom fireflies zipped past my study window. It was written in a passion and could do with calming down somewhat. But, to be truthful, I don't want to calm it down!

❝ Today, on the last day of April 2003, I completed my 500th poem, (appropriately entitled 'Landfill'), precisely 31 months after beginning this mad odyssey back in October of 2000. One would have to be inhuman not to do the arithmetic.

In something like 930 days I have hammered away for four hours a day at five hundred sonnets, sestinas, villanelles, quatrains, pantoums, odes, nursery rhymes and every other species of the verse tribe known to me. It has been a journey unlike any other in a not exactly sheltered life. And yet I do not begrudge a single one of the 223,000 minutes devoted (so my calculator informs me) to this new and utterly consuming passion.

So what has all this 'scribble, scribble scribble' achieved?

When my publishers set the print run of *A Glass Half Full* at ten thousand copies last year, there were those in the book publishing business who thought

Hutchinson must be mad. No-one sells ten thousand copies of an original book of verse in the UK. Nor has it been done, as far as I can discover, for many years.

But Sue Freestone, the publishing director of Hutchinson, was right, and all the naysayers were wrong. Every book was sold and *A Glass Half Full* is being reprinted. Original poetry can still sell in decent quantities in Britain, as I always secretly believed. But my word, dear readers, if only you knew what a kerfuffle such a sale has made in certain incestuous literary circles.

It may 'not be a level playing field' as one poet sniffed to me recently while gulping down half a bottle of my best Chambertin. But what aspect of life is? Money, notoriety and curiosity value have their uses. Could it be that it is now some of the older generation poets, bunkered in what Tom Wolfe, the American novelist and critic, calls 'the poor old mallarme'd and ezrapounded world of contemporary poetry', who find themselves perhaps a little out of joint? Even (whisper it, softly) a little out of date?

Certainly the success of a book of rhymed verse in traditional forms appears to have discomforted one or two of them. A well-known British poet confided to *The Wall Street Journal* newspaper recently that while the author of *A Glass Half Full* continues to write 'rhyming verse' he will remain a 'Philistine' and can never be a 'true poet'.

This is an odd accusation when he knows perfectly well that thousands of you have been kind enough to attend my poetry readings from Brighton to Glasgow. What were all of us doing for two or three hours at those events then, Mr. Well-Known-British-Poet — *pretending* to listen to poetry?

And why would the Royal Shakespeare Company invite me to join their actors on the stage of the Swan Theatre, reading from *A Glass Half Full* to a packed house, if we weren't about the business of poetry? And what were the folk in the audience doing standing on their hind legs — were they busy applauding '*false* poetry'? And what was the RNIB and the National Library for the Blind doing translating *A Glass Half Full* into braille and talking-book editions— are their editors, too, all 'Philistines'?

What our Well-Known-British-Poet possibly meant to say is that he has no time for people who enjoy an evening of poetry that 'rollicks and rolls with rhyme, meter and melody,' to quote Tom Wolfe again. Well, that's his bad luck. True poetry is surely in the mind of the reader or listener. Free verse has no monopoly on that. No one person, school or institution can lay claim to judge what is 'true poetry'.

Whether it is T.S. Eliot at his most impenetrable or Francis Thompson at a Lord's cricket match; Larkin in a morbid funk or Frost mending a recalcitrant wall; Charlotte Mew with her bride in the attic or Les Murray on his milk lorry — surely the cathedral of English poetry, which is itself one of the wonders of the civilised world, is a broad enough church to embrace any and all forms of verse?

Name-calling and ridiculous disputes about form have been with us since Palaeolithic artists daubed ochre beauty on the walls of caves— they are nothing new. But an art form which too often appears to despise its potential audience, an art form in which — in the words of David Lee, the editor of *The Jackdaw* — 'anything traditional is considered backward and populist, whilst anything unconventional is intellectual and challenging,' can hardly complain about poor sales and lack of public appreciation. Or level playing fields, for that matter.

Surely it is the quality of the work itself, not the form in which it is presented, that should concern us. What counts, is whether work touches us, amuses us, entertains us or moves us. Throwing rocks at any artist whose work is heartfelt is bad enough. But traducing literary work which others patently enjoy smacks of intellectual bankruptcy and the rage of an emperor discovered naked on his own city streets.

If there are emperors without clothes in the world of contemporary poetry, they are more likely to be disguised as those who insist that it is the *general reader* who is to blame for the fact that they can barely understand half of what is written and less of what was meant. Or else, it will be those who hold that poetry is, by definition, an exclusive art— where 'any poem that can be understood in less than four read-throughs' is mere doggerel.

It is undeniable that a great many poets for the past three-quarters of a century have been gripped in the opaque thrall of T.S. Eliot and Ezra Pound. Both these men may have been geniuses at what they did— although I will happily admit that some of Pound's later work resists all my efforts to understand what he is saying. Nor can anyone deny that much of what followed in the wake of Pound and Eliot left millions of readers feeling that either we must be 'Philistines' indeed, or that we have somehow missed the point of it all. To quote one of my own poems (a detestable and ungentlemanly habit, granted):

> I wish you'd write for _us_, my dear.
> It's lonely for us, waiting here.
> I wish your gifts adorned our shelves
> Instead of writing for yourselves.

For myself, I will continue to write verse not because I wish to, but because I am compelled to. I am perfectly aware that this makes me appear ridiculous to some. I am aware, too, that it is changing me from a minor media mogul into.... well, into exactly what, I do not yet know. Perhaps I should have started all this thirty years ago, instead of building up a fortune no sane man could ever spend. It was fun, making all that money— but not as much fun as writing poetry! ""

And now, I must thank you, dear reader. Hundreds of you have already written to me with your criticisms, congratulations and advice. I have therefore set up a website where you can post messages if you wish, check tour dates, listen to poems being read or watch video clips filmed at various readings. I may not be able to reply to every message you leave, but you can be certain that I will read it!

As a refugee from thirty years at the coal face of commerce, you cannot know what a thrill it is to do this little thing. To write and perform verse for an appreciative audience. If you experience even a fraction of the pleasure in reading these poems that I have derived from writing them, then I could ask for no more. Thank you. Thank you so very much.

Dorsington
June, 2004

The web site address for readers to post comments, find tour dates, or listen and view spoken word and video clips is: **www.felixdennis.com**

Author's Note

The poems in *Lone Wolf* were written between June 2002 and March 2004. The reader will find, in tiny type, clues to where they were written: Soho (Kingly Street, London); Dorsington (a village in Warwickshire); Candlewood (a lakeside community in Connecticut); New York (49th Street and 2nd Avenue, Manhattan); and Mustique (an island in the West Indies).

For a prolific author, the choice of which poems to include in a book is a vexed subject. Vexing for the author, that is! Simon Rae, my editor, and Moni Mannings, who kindly reads virtually all my poems, both weigh in with numerous criticisms and suggestions. We have yet to come to blows, but it is a fraught process — albeit the final choice is mine. Should you wish to read a few of the poems excluded from this book, feel free to check out **www.felixdennis.com.**

Lastly, I have received comments from readers concerning differences between the spoken-word readings of poems on the CD in the back of my books and the printed version. These differences arise because I record the poems months prior to publication. In nearly all cases, the printed version is the 'correct' one — although, as a famous American poet once noted, no poem is ever completely finished; it is merely abandoned.

LONE WOLF

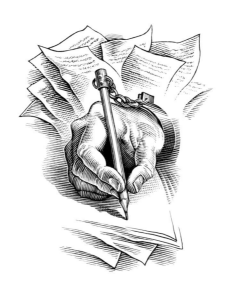

Diplomacy

Two blind men stand within a darkened room,
   Unmanned, unarmed, their fear as thick as night;
Each certain that the other seeks his doom,
   Each boasting of his knife, and new found sight.

[DORSINGTON]

The Summer of Love

['If you can remember the sixties, you weren't really there.'] — *Jerry Rubin*

We were clappy-happy, we were hippy-dippy —
We were building Eden by the mighty Mississippi.
We were very certain, we were very sure,
We were very righteous, (and we were very poor),
And we scolded non-believers and we taunted the police,
And our women made us tea while we puffed the pipes of peace.

We were sappy-happy, we were hippy trippy —
We were building Eden by the mighty Mississippi.
We were dressed in satin, army coats and beads,
And we sat cross-legged while we sorted stems and seeds,
And we swapped each others' lovers and our hair grew wild and woolly,
And our rooms reeked of joss and our women of patchouli.

We were clappy-happy, we were hippy-dippy —
We were building Eden by the mighty Mississippi.
And we lived in San Francisco, or else in Notting Hill,
And we made a lot of babies though our women took the pill,
And we played a lot of Zappa and Dylan and the 'Dead,
And we talked a lot — but mostly I've forgotten what we said.

[DORSINGTON]

(with apologies to Edna St. Vincent Millay)

'A lie fills up the world...'

'A lie fills up the world before the truth puts on its coat',
    For naked lies leave leaden truth behind;
All falsehoods breed a fever for lack of antidote,
    While error strives to emulate its kind.

A lie will batter blindly till its barb has struck a mark,
    While truth is quivered up in bitter joy;
Truth knows itself a candle held aloft against the dark,
    It may not replicate what lies destroy.

Some liars lie unknowing, seeking but to entertain,
    Their gossip idle offspring of their mirth,
Forgetful that such rumour sows a thistle-field of pain,
    A hostage to the hybrid of its birth.

'A lie fills up the world before the truth is up and dressed',
    For truth sleeps late, its conscience clear as sky;
Yet conscience is but armour, built for steady pace, at best:
    And lies sprout wings, the better yet to fly.

[MUSTIQUE]

[5]

Silly Seasons

This is the weather an editor likes,
      And so do I;
When the rag is full of gossip and strikes,
      And sales are high;
And a train derails for want of a brake,
And drunk celebrities drown in a lake,
And ministers' wives are burned at the stake,
And readers laugh 'til their bellies ache,
      And so do I.

This is the weather the editors fear,
      And so do I;
When the rag is flat as yesterday's beer,
      And twice as dry;
And no-one has called another man 'LIAR!',
And nobody murders some lass in the choir,
And markets are quiet for seller and buyer,
And readers hurl the rag in the fire,
      And so do I!

[DORSINGTON]

(with apologies to Thomas Hardy)

'All living words are creatures...'

All living words are creatures of their kind,
Each tribe of scent and sound proscribed by sense;
Some sultans in their palace, some consigned
To wander in the desert with their tents.
A *snout* is not a *mouth*, nor *lips* a *beak*,
And *pus* has little place in words of praise,
If *shit* squats close to *wit*, they barely speak;
If youth's *uncouth*, then *truth* must look both ways.
Their author gods may use them as they will —
Fierce nomads make a novelty in towns,
But soon outstay their welcome. Pomp sits ill
With courtiers as verbs or clowns as nouns.
    When poet shepherds come the great *iamb*,
    Then restless sleeps the *lion* with the *lamb*!

[DORSINGTON]

'The words of a living language are like creatures...' begins Morris Bishop in his marvelous essay
'Good Usage, Bad Usage, and Usage' prefacing *The American Heritage Dictionary of the English
Language*. His words of wisdom are worth the price of that worthy, if somewhat stuffy, tome alone.

23 Roads

[On the 50th anniversary of Watson and Crick's
discovery of the structure of DNA]

Here is the code of codes,
Here are the maps of riven fate.
Here is the parting of roads,
Here is the kingdom, here the gate.

Here is the clue of clues,
Here are the paths where none have trod.
Here is the alchemist's fuse,
Here are the hieroglyphics of God.

Here is the womb of wombs,
Here is the pit where life drew breath.
Here is the coil of dooms,
Here is the cradle of birth and death.

Here is the book of books,
Here is the prisoner, here the cell.
Here are the torturer's hooks:
Here are the 23 roads to hell.

[MUSTIQUE]

'We've discovered the secret of life.'
— *Francis Crick in The Eagle pub, Cambridge, February 28, 1953.*

That he had. Along with James Watson, Crick had made 'possibly the greatest scientific discovery of all time' — the structure of DNA. Here was the long sought Book of Life, packaged in twenty-three separate pairs of chromosomes, a codebook written in symbols of four chemical letters less than a few trillionths of an inch long. Watson and Crick's discovery changed everything, for better and for worse, for good and for evil. Nothing could ever now be the same. Our tinkerings in nuclear fission might be compared to the power of DNA to 'alter everything' by imagining a Palaeolithic spear hurled at a Stealth bomber. One thing is certain, there will be tears before bedtime, and all the legislation from every court, Parliament, Congress or Diet in the world will be powerless to prevent it.

Advice To Any Daughter

Dearest, men are fools and know it.
Do not blame them overmuch —
Nor is it thought kind to show it
When it comes to love and such.

Bite your tongue and hide your laughter,
Though you read them like a book;
There is but one thing they're after
(Til they need a nurse or cook).

Charming, yes, but helpless babies,
Never buy one on a whim;
Test it first for lice or rabies —
Only then 'give in' to him.

Dearest, men are fools and know it.
One last thing before you go:
Make exception for a poet —
They, at least, know what *you* know!

[DORSINGTON]

'I built myself a house of wood...'

I built myself a house of wood
Where once an apple orchard stood.
On stormy nights I lay in bed
While rafters moaned above my head.

They wept aloud for limbs long lost,
For buds pinched out by early frost,
For wicker baskets piled with fruit,
For phantom branch and withered root.

I caulked the roof and rafter beams,
But still they whispered in my dreams,
They spoke of rising sap and wood:
— And then, at last, I understood.

This spring I planted out a score
Of apple saplings by my door.
Now stormy nights my rafters chime
To cider choirs and nursery-rhyme.

[MUSTIQUE]

Tempus Fugit

*[A gentleman arrives with a complaint at
Father Time's office and accosts a receptionist]*

Sure, some mistake has happened here,
   Old Father Time has lost the score —
I went to bed nineteen, my dear,
   And woke to find me forty-four!

Come, all may make mistake, (in truth,
   Most paper-work is but a bore).
Bid Father Time give back my youth —
   We'll call it quits and say no more.

Perhaps he just mislaid the file,
   You'll find it there behind a drawer.
(Go slip it in the youngster's pile
   From anything through twenty-four.)

Your master bids me *'go away'*?
   He says he's *'heard all this before'*?
I went to bed eighteen, I say —
   And woke to find me fifty-four!

See here, my dear there's some mistake;
   I'll not be shown the bloody door!
Go ask again, for pity's sake —
   I'm seventeen — not sixty-four!

An English Light

9:45 on a fine June night,
I watch from the window and write and write
As the fields are lit by the red-eyed flight
Of the westering sun — as the trees ignite,
And the shadows lance in the slanted light,
Each leaf a halo of fire, more bright
Than the pale moon clothed in mottle and white
Awaiting the arms of her purple knight.

Little is moving in Eden this night
But the ears of an owl on a branchy height
For the rustle of voles, however slight,
As a martin blurs like a sickle kite
Of gunmetal grey... and I write and write
This hymn of delight in an English light.

[DORSINGTON]

[13]

Answered Prayers

I have met truth in the mouth of liars,
    And joy in a season of fear:
Be certain of your heart's desires,
    And cautious what you pray for, dear.

I have seen love in the eyes of whores,
    And truth in a bully's sneer.
The hopes of men have hidden claws:
    Be cautious what you hope for, dear.

I have known pain in the jests of friends
    And wit in a drunkard's tear,
Whatever you wish for— life amends:
    Be cautious what you wish for, dear.

[DORSINGTON]

EC Directive 3923/ 94645687342-9045888

Withdrawals of labour, formerly known as 'stoppages'
Are prohibited — as are all so-called 'jury trials';
As are those food-stuffs formerly known as 'sausages'
In the islands formerly known as the 'British Isles'.

[DORSINGTON]

[14]

Dead Man's Shoes

"Move on over, rover —
Don't you know you're done?
Can't you read the writing on the wall?
Check the vista, mister —
Clock the setting sun;
Getting kind of late for you to stall.

"Time to muster, buster —
Time to fade away,
Lot of good men here parked on the beach.
Smell the roses, Moses —
Each dog has his day,
Take the goddam watch and make a speech."

Pushy young turks are impatient for news,
Young Cinderellas are singing the blues,
Wannabees, just like you used to be... Choose!
Whose gonna fill this dead man's shoes?

[MUSTIQUE]

' The flowers of desire...'

The flowers of desire from our youth,
  (Those thistle seeds of waking and obsession),
Lie scattered by the harvesters of truth,
  And perish in the winter of possession.

[MUSTIQUE]

'When slattern Darkness...'

When slattern Darkness lifts her skirt
  To couple with Despair,
Her bastard offspring, Shame and Hurt,
  Are shunted down the stair;
They wander in the streets to squirt
  Graffiti as they cry:
"Our mum's a slut. I'm Shame. He's Hurt.
  We'll find you, by and by."

[MUSTIQUE]

Where the Rain Comes From in Senegal

Each drop of rain was once a soul in sin,
  Hell's demons spit them out in lieu of rent;
They drum upon our roofs of mud and tin,
  Reminding unbelievers to repent!

But what of those who lived by His commands
  And loved the Lord and never told a lie?
God's plan was they should water desert sands
  As angels' tears— but angels never cry.

[MUSTIQUE]

'That country has its joys...'

["I'll die young, but it's like kissing God..."] — *Lenny Bruce*

That country has its joys, though fierce and short,
A hammered heartbeat leaping in the breast;
The certainty of bliss, if dearly bought,
Sure shelter from the storm through time compressed.
'ABANDON HOPE...' Yes, yes — we read the signs,
Those stony words of wisdom from the wise,
The mantra down the years from Philistines
Who slop their beer while neighbours roll their eyes.
And now I know why snipers never speak
Of war or wounds. They think of those who fell;
The pull of dreams where death plays hide-and-seek:
The peaks of Darien, the bowels of hell.
   I loved that country once and sometimes yearn
   To taste its air again — and not return.

[MUSTIQUE]

Portable Darkness

A trapped fly scuds against a window pane
   While at its back a door is standing wide;
So men conspire to seek the light in vain —
   Their darkness but the cloak of human pride.

[DORSINGTON]

'Are our presses rolling...'

"Are our presses rolling
    Like thunder on the run,
The giant reels still spinning
    Now I'm dead, my son?"

"Aye, the presses thunder,
    The reels are larger now,
The circulation's way up;
    Best you don't know how."

"Are the headlines screaming
    In type as black as sin,
And do our rivals weaken —
    You'd never let them win?"

"Aye, the type is blacker,
        Four colour now — the best!
We whittled down the linens
        And bought up half the rest."

"Are the worms still squirming
        That covet No.10,
Ministers still toadying
        And leaking like a pen?"

"Aye, they leak like buckets
        With bottoms full of shot;
But now we breed 'celebrities'
        To fatten for the pot."

"Are our readers baying
        For foreigner and Jew;
Do we still pay no taxes,
        And slander fools who do?"

"Aye, we finger scapegoats,
        But that's not down to me;
The minute you ceased breathing —
        I sold the company!"

[MUSTIQUE]

Lovers of A E Housman will know immediately where the form for this poem originates. 'Is My Team Ploughing' is one of my favourite from his first collection, *A Shropshire Lad*, published in 1896. The world waited 26 years before he published another. My lawyers have asked me to state categorically that this poem in no way represents or is an allusion to or is based upon the character of any press baron, living or dead. I affirm what must surely be obvious to any discerning reader.

The Caravan Moves On

Friends die — and we screw our wet eyes up,
    And swear we'll miss them now they're gone.
We mourn — then Arsenal win the Cup,
    Dogs bark, but the caravan moves on.

[DORSINGTON]

The last line comes from an old Turkish proverb. It is also the title of a small classic of travel
literature by Irfan Orga published in 1958, which describes the author's short stay with nomads
in the High Taurus mountains of central Turkey. Republished recently in an abridged edition by
Eland Books, it is a haunting description of a lost world.   Perfect for armchair travellers— as are
many other books in the Eland catalogue.

The Comrade's Cat

The Comrade's cat lies curled upon a chair —
A weathered chair whose leather once was red,
Where yellow eyes return its master's stare;

A stare that grinds the Comrades to despair,
A stare from which all pity has been bled.
The Comrade's cat lies curled upon a chair,

A chair within a prissy, book lined lair,
A chair where men have sat in fumbling dread,
Where yellow eyes return a scholar's stare.

Neat piles of paper conjured from the air,
Long lists of traitors — soon to join the dead;
Their Comrade's cat lies curled upon a chair,

Awaiting Nadya's footsteps on the stair.
Fat Cheka knows that — soon! — he will be fed.
Bright yellow eyes return an exile's stare,

Who folds his napkin, like his lists, with care;
Prefers his meat served rare on black rye bread.
The Comrade's cat lies curled upon a chair —
Where yellow eyes return a madman's stare.

[MUSTIQUE]

The 20th century produced more than its fair share of ideological mass killers. Hitler and Stalin, of course, leap to mind. As does Mao-Tse Tung. But Lenin? Surely not. Surely Joseph Stalin twisted Marxist-Leninism into his own looking-glass landscape of show trials, Gulags, ethnic murder and repressive madness? That would have been my own shrugged reaction, until recently. But as modern Russia opens long sealed vaults describing its Soviet descent into hell, the record shows that it was Lenin who again and again urged the army, the Commisars and Politburo to use "the absolute maximum of violence and terror than can be conceived to utterly eradicate counter-revolutionary forces." Scores of his directives were so violent in language, so appalling in their intent, that they were kept from public view for over seventy years. Here's an example: "Comrades! The insurrection of five kulak districts must be pitilessly suppressed. Hang a hundred. Hang a thousand. But hang them in full view!" Yes he loved cats (and kept one I have called 'Cheka', after the political police, in his Kremlin office). Yes he was a brilliant intellectual. And he adored children. But he was also a sick, demented deathmonger who believed that an iota of mercy shown to an enemy was the highest form of treason. This is the same fastidious man who walked the corridors of the Kremlin turning off lights at night to save electricity. Who sharpened his pencils obsessively every day. And who always killed at second hand. Truly, Lenin was Stalin's mentor.

Hunting Monsters

[A shanty for the US Department of Homeland Security]

We fish them up from murky seas
    As orcas hunt a porpoise,
We shape our hooks from liberties,
    The oars from habeus corpus.

Like Ahab on some phantom quest,
    We flee where few pursue us,
We lecture friends who loved us best,
    And spit on those who knew us.

In grief and rage we flense our cause,
    No mercy and no quarter;
Harpooning laws on foreign shores,
    Their oil the spoil of slaughter.

Some songs are older than the Ark,
    And, if you wish, I'll hum one:
When hunting monsters in the dark,
Take care, lest you become one.

[MUSTIQUE]

'He who fights with monsters might take care lest he thereby become a monster.' — Friedrich Nietzsche, *Jenseits von Gut und Böse* (1886)

Good Morning!

Having spilt all the milk while tearing the tamper-proof perforated plastic ring with my teeth from the plastic bottle (there being insufficient purchase on said ring) I then managed to cut two of my fingertips badly (most probably contracting botulism as I did so) whilst grappling with the vacuum pack sealed-for-full-freshness semi-rigid container containing eight rashers of prime low-fat bacon. The kitchen counter resembles an abattoir. Convenience foods will be the death of us.

[SOHO]

[23]

Brownie Points
[On Coming Across a Photograph of My Father and Myself as a Baby]

I never knew that smile,
   Nor touched that hand,
Flash frozen as he scoops the golden sand
   From moat to pile.

His arms are out of reach
   The snapshot blurred,
My chubby face stares vacant and absurd
   Upon some beach.

He flew — as cuckoos do,
   And lost his sons;
All children boast of fathers, savings ones
   They never knew.

[MUSTIQUE]

Kodak box-cameras used to be called 'Brownies'. Perhaps I should have called this 'Brownie Points...and Clicks'. I assume the photograph was taken by my mother just prior to my brother being born. My father left us, never to return, a year or so later.

To Fellow Travellers

I shall not view the Taj Mahal,
Or ride where Lawrence rode,
I shall not vault a turtle's back,
Nor stride where Darwin strode.

The Road to Oxiana's dust
Shall hoard its mystery,
Samoan chiefs in Levi jeans
Shall sell no shells to me.

I seek a world without the world
Since first I wrote in rhyme,
For those who care — a bulletin
May come, from time to time.

[DORSINGTON]

'What *Ulysses* is to the novel... and what *The Waste Land* is to poetry, [Robert Byron's] *The Road to Oxiana* is to the travel book.' — William Dalrymple, *The Guardian Review*

We Are Now Too Many

They fell the trees, and watch the desert grow,
    And mothers sell their children for a penny.
We write a cheque, but in our hearts we know
    The simple truth: that we are now too many.

Yet who can blame a man for chopping wood?
    The nights are cold, and families need feeding.
We write a cheque and pray it does some good.
    The famine wanes... an interval for breeding.

And who could blame a man for wanting sons?
    Or wanting better housing than a sewer?
We write a cheque, the warlords buy some guns,
    And in the sea the fish are growing fewer,

While trawler nets are bursting at the seams;
    We save the whales, for fear there shan't be any.
We write a cheque, but in our restless dreams
    A demon sings— that we are now too many.

[MUSTIQUE]

Nobody had a good word to say of Thomas Malthus during the 'green revolution' that tripled harvest yields in many parts of the Third World in the 20th century. And recent scientific advances promise even better news for hungry humanity with genetically-modified crops. So why did I write these gloomy and (to me, at least,) disturbing lines? Because in my heart of hearts I believe that much of what the West contributes in aid does far, far more harm than good. Because the Lords of Aid, as that excellent reporter, Michael Buerk of the BBC, calls them, have a vested interest in the status quo. Because, as in Ethiopia, our aid has turned an entire nation into 'a country of beggars'. We cannot stop writing the cheques because we know no alternative... and images of starving children haunt our sleep. But Malthus was right. A species that refuses to limit its population will eventually have it limited for it — in the most brutal, catastrophic way.

Wages

The wages of living are riddled with qualms
And are paid in a spadeful of soil.

The wages of labour are dock leaf balms
To poultice the poison of toil.

The wages of bliss in a lover's arms
Are blubbering brats you adore.

The wages of sin you will find in the Psalms —
Or nailed on a whorehouse door.

The wages of tossing a beggar alms
Are dependent on what you intend;

But the wages that harvest a thousand salaams
Are reaped in the heart of a friend.

[DORSINGTON]

'Coming — Ready or Not!'

Though science says a thing may not be done
　　Because the cage of light is fixed by law,
Yet men *shall* warp their way from sun to sun,
　　'To boldly go where no man went before'.

Tool-makers, planet-breakers, nature's bane,
　　A mad god's instrument to wake the dead;
We did it once and shall, by Christ, again;
　　And if not us— devices in our stead.

Our lives the polished mirrors of our craft,
　　Each failure but a signpost to the sun —
My God, how Galileo would have laughed
　　To hear them witter on: '*It <u>can't</u> be done!*'

[DORSINGTON]

"**warp factor** (in science fiction) the degree to which the velocity of a spaceship etc. exceeds that of light; usu. with numeral, as warp factor 8 etc." — *Shorter Oxford English Dictionary* (2002 edition)

"To boldly go where no man went before..." — '*Star Trek*' television series created by Gene Roddenbury

"This 'telephone' has too many shortcomings to be seriously considered as a means of communication. The device is inherently of no value to us." — Western Union internal memo, 1876

"Who the hell wants to hear actors talk?" — H.M. Warner, Warner Brothers, 1927

"Heavier-than-air flying machines are impossible." — Lord Kelvin, president, Royal Society, 1895

"Louis Pasteur's theory of germs is ridiculous fiction." — Pierre Pachet, Professor of Physiology at Toulouse, 1872

"If I had thought about it, I wouldn't have done the experiment. The literature was full of examples that said you can't do this." — Spencer Silver, creator of 3-M's "Post-It" Notes

"I think there's a world market for about five computers." — Thomas J. Watson, founder of IBM.

'Any fool can filch a smile...'

Any fool can filch a smile
To paste upon a door,
Any fool can cache a pile
Of sins beneath the floor;

Any fool can bolt a heart
And hide away the key,
Any fool can plot a chart
Or sail away to sea;

But boards will sag
   And smiles will slip
      With nothing to hold them fast,
And bolts will rust
   And the bravest ship
      Must straggle to port at last.

[SOHO]

French Connection

[for M-F]

We do not speak as lovers,
Nor hold each other's hand;
We give no sign to others,
To help them understand.
Nor have we planned
To meet each other's mothers.

I play the ukulele,
She solos in the choir;
Our countries quarrel daily
And call each other liar.
And yet the fire
Burns brightly— even gaily.

I tell her, 'I adore you,'
She pouts and pokes her tongue.
Well, that's French women for you,
But once the harp is strung
No song is sung
More gently to restore you.

I sit and write my verses,
She sips a glass of wine
And shrugs at grumpy curses,
She's here in every line,
This book of mine
Is graced by her sweet mercies.

[DORSINGTON]

'Downsizing'

The firm's alive with murmurs,
The thrum of gossips din,
The sneers of old long-termers —
Whoever's out — they're in.

No parachutes or rip-cords,
No lifebuoys as she dives,
Fat bastards with their clipboards
Are sharpening their knives.

Receptionists are tearful,
The Boss averts his eye,
'H.R.' is grimly cheerful —
But then — they're paid to lie.

It's meeting, every minute,
It's tackle, grapple, block!
It's 'keep yer 'ead down', innit?
It's in by eight o'clock!

It's straining blood and sinew
To keep abreast of moves:
"The hangings will continue
— Until morale improves!"

[MUSTIQUE]

[32]

Caribbean Christmas

Beside a gaudy Christmas tree
I polish off a g and t;
The hotel's fine. I watch the sea
Roll up to picture-postcard palms
And smear the sun-cream on my arms.

Behind me, air conditioned hums
Drown out the mirth of boozy chums:
'A *toast!*' The clink of coke and rums.
A raffish lizard's rolling eye
Surveys an irritating fly —

Its tongue darts out! An airy blur,
And then we're both back where we were
With neither of a mind to stir,
Surrounded by banana fronds
And golden koi in concrete ponds.

Two men in khaki cross the sand,
A walkie-talkie in each hand.
I turn to watch a local band
Play carols just outside the fence,
While guests toss coins in recompense.

'*Good King Wenceslas looked out...*
'*As the snow lay round about...*'
The music stops. The guards, no doubt,
Have shooed them on their merry way
From paradise, this Christmas Day.

[MUSTIQUE]

In all fairness, I should make it clear that while these lines were composed on Mustique, they refer to a vacation taken years ago at an international resort on another Caribbean island. There are no fences or razor-wire on Mustique's beaches. Nor do armed security guards lord it over the local population. We have our problems, as does any community, but huge amounts of co-operative effort and money continue to be spent on Mustique in what amounts to a unique social experiment between home-owners and the St. Vincent & the Grenadines government.

Early Morning in Dorsington

The cows stand silent in the fields
Their soft mouths filled with grass and dew,
White mist is rolling down the ridge,
The eggshell sky is milky blue.

Two ducks have landed on the lawn;
My old black cat has caught a doe —
Not badly hurt — I force a thumb
In Moushka's mouth and let her go.

A blackbird struts upon the hedge,
His warbling fit to stir the Bard,
Who, so they say, once walked this way —
(In Warwickshire, old myths die hard).

The swallows wheel in search of mud,
My bed is made, the cat is fed,
And I must down to London town,
Where fools like me must earn their bread.

[DORSINGTON]

Prodigal Friend

I heard my name
And turned and saw
A face I'd never
Seen before —
And then I got it!
Big wide grin,
With arms stretched out to
Hug me in —

My heart leapt up
In foolish joy,
And the years dissolved:
'My dear, dear boy!'
As we stood there grinning,
Eye to eye,
My mates embarrassed —
What cared I?

At last I turned
To make amend,
And the words choked out:
'My oldest friend...'
And we talked while time
Wore out its knife —
My prodigal friend,
My friend for life.

[CANDLEWOOD]

Thirty years after I had last seen him, an old school friend and cross-country running mate, walked up to me out of the blue at a poetry reading in St. James's Square, London. For just an instant, the carapace of time dissolved. Of all traits in the human psyche, perhaps friendship, rather than love or self-preservation, is both the most enduring and the most noble part of us — untainted as it is by the *quid pro quo* of family ties, sex, or financial dependency. Odd, too, how the heart and mind instantly reforge such old friendships, no matter how many years have passed since their last renewal.

Laughing Buddha

Laughing Buddha in the sand,
Spade and bucket in your hand,
Newly-minted, wonder-eyed,
Architect of time and tide;

Mischief written on your brow,
Master of the here-and-now,
Free of past and future's taint,
Life the canvas, joy the paint;

Sorcerer of sea and sky,
Innocent of where or why,
Flesh and stone in symmetry —
Wanting nothing but to *be*;

Offspring of a dream deferred,
Fill your bucket; speak no word!
Hoard your secrets; stop your ears!
Alphabets spell only tears;

You who sit in Eden's shade,
Teasing angels with your spade,
Empty-headed, eyes of blue —
We were once as wise as you;

Infant Buddha, sifting sand,
All creation in your hand,
Where does infant wisdom fly?
Only heaven knows — not I.

[MUSTIQUE]

I was rereading Peter Matthiessen's limpid sojourn into Buddhism and Nepal, *The Snow Leopard*, and had reached a chapter of his musings on holy men who live only in the here and now (or *Now!*) as he puts it — having attained sufficient wisdom to see through the camouflage of past and future — when it occurred to me that such a creature was right in front of me. A toddler furiously digging on the beach, oblivious to his surroundings, utterly content with his lot and not a thought in his head but to dig, dig, dig!. Even the (apparent) uselessness of his self-appointed task fitted Matthiessen's glorious description of epiphany-in-action. I scratched the first four lines of 'Laughing Buddha' in the sand with a stick — having neglected to bring a pencil with me. By next morning, only 'Architect of time and tide' had survived the waves' incursions.

Nothing Is Lost
[A Charm of Retrieval]

Nothing is lost, save to the seeker;
Nothing is missing, save for its worth;
Nothing is hidden, save to the hunter;
Memory's mysteries litter the earth.

Nothing is gone, save for the moment;
Nothing is covered, save for the ken;
Nothing is forfeit, save to its keeper;
Mother of muses— show me again.

[DORSINGTON]

Our Neighbours

'Of fur and feather, scale and shell,
Those neighbours we consign to hell...'

They use no jails, except those built by men,
   No management, no coin, no entourage;
They rest content, while we must stalk the world,
   Our so-called sentience, mere camouflage.
We lack their speed, their balance and their sight;
   The skill of merely being what we are
Has long been lost to us. But not to them!
   They make community, but pass no jar
Among themselves to drown the gods of wrath.
   They do no ill, far less do they conspire
To pox the world with gulags — or with slaves;
   Not one has ever sought a man for hire.

They foul no earth, they scorch no forest black;
   And if they kill, they feed upon the lame.
They scourge no lakes, nor fill the sea with wrack.
   They mate beneath the sun and not in shame;
They bind the world — mysterious, in such ways
   As we have yet to learn or understand.
They dig no graves, nor mines. They scar no hills.
   They bear no toxic gifts to blight the land.
They know no guilt — nor have they reason to —
   If courtesy could salvage men's despite,
Have they not paid due ransom? Search your heart:
   Their beauty is a child's chief delight.

[MUSTIQUE]

Fire Inside

Some have come like moths to flame —
They sense the fires inside you;
A few to reignite their shame,
And some to lie beside you.

Some have come to douse the coals
As volunteers, in batches;
Some with ladders, tea and rolls;
And some with oil and matches.

Some have come from warmer lands
To speak of frozen roses;
Some with hatchets in their hands,
And some with swollen hoses.

Some have come through smoke and mist
To wonder at the crater;
But I have come — an arsonist —
My heart — a detonator.

[DORSINGTON]

[39]

Upon Julia's Bolts

I rummaged last night within Julia's Clothes
While musing on Herrick — how sweetly flows
That lecherous pen among buttons and bows.

Yet what should he make of a Tracy who preens
With bolts in her belly, scarce out of her teens,
Three henna tattoos, Doc Martens and jeans?

[NEW YORK]

Robert 'Gather ye rosebuds while ye may' Herrick (1591-1674) wrote often of Julia and very often of clothes, as in the poem 'Sweet Disorder' which starts 'A sweet disorder in the dress / Kindles in clothes a wantonness...' The lines above were sparked by another of his sly winks:

Upon Julia's Clothes

Whenas in silks my Julia goes,
Then, then, methinks, how sweetly flows
That liquefaction of her clothes!

Next, when I cast mine eyes and see
That brave vibration each way free,
—O how that glittering taketh me!

Jack and Jill

Jack and Jill went up the hill
    To fetch a pail of water;
Jack fell down and broke his crown
    And Jill came tumbling after.

Jill sued Jack and Jack sued back,
    The judge is going to fine her;
Now the pail's been sent to jail
    For abandoning a minor.

We'll sue Jack and he'll sue Jill,
    The hill is suing for scandal;
The water says he'll sue the press —
    And everyone's suing the handle.

[MUSTIQUE]

Many Roads

There stretch as many roads
    To heaven as to hell —
While zealots brandish wrath,
    Example casts its spell.

For one good woman's love
    Or sinner's sage advice,
Does more to heal the world
    Than threats of paradise.

If men be truly damned,
    The wise possess no keys —
Their narrow paths are crammed
    With homeless refugees.

How many martyr's stakes
    Would craft a Noah's Ark?
We each, by separate paths,
    Must journey to the dark.

Friend, teach no single truth
    Of prophet, book or bell —
There stretch as many roads
    To heaven as to hell.

[MUSTIQUE]

I am privileged to employ one of the finest journalists in America. His name is Bill Falk, the editor-in-chief of the US edition of *The Week*. Every week he is allocated just 200 words or so in a little red box on page 5 of *The Week* for his Editor's Letter. Quite frankly, it is an astonishing tour-de-force of condensed erudition, common sense, dry wit and sly wisdom. The lines above were inspired by his Editor's Letter for the January 10th, 2003 edition in which he wrote: "My own view is that this perversion of religious faith comes from the calcification of great teachings into narrow-minded dogma. Instead of meeting people's real spiritual yearnings, too many holy men teach that there is but one, highly exclusive, road to Truth."

Haunted

When I was but a child,
The dark was full of dread,
I trembled then as monsters filed
To loom beside my bed.

The shadows on the wall
Hid creeping, crawling eyes,
The curtain ghost was six foot tall,
The wardrobe full of sighs.

Yet grown to man's estate,
My cupboards full of tears,
Awake at nights I know the weight
Of wasted, selfish years.

And ogres on the stairs
Must blush at what they built,
Or wet themselves on angry chairs
By mirrors filled with guilt.

[MUSTIQUE]

Tonight, We Dance

Here is a word from a man who used too many;
 Here is a the hand of a man who lived by touch;
Here is the compound interest from one penny —
 At seven percent — is a buck and half too much?

One dollar and forty odd cents, bar all dispersals;
 One hundred and forty times the capital sum
From three score years of shabby old dress rehearsals,
 And a promise of starring roles at Kingdom Come?

Come leap by the light of a moon which wanes and waxes;
 Come howl in the shadow of Enron's neon glance;
Dear Christ, the little you save they steal in taxes.
 Come, take my hand, my friend: tonight, we dance!

[NEW YORK]

Unwanted Miracle

 The filter in the pond is packed with snails,
 I scoop them out and plop them by a fern.
 The older goldfish sneer and flick their tails;
 As soon as God has left, the snails return.

[MUSTIQUE]

Strangers

This stranger stood before you
    Has known you all your life:
This stranger is your mother,
    Your brother or your wife.

Your sister's eyes are mirrors,
    Your father's face a mask,
Their answers pre-recorded —
    So none but strangers ask.

The hearts of men lie hidden,
    The many and the one:
This stranger is your daughter,
    Your husband or your son.

[DORSINGTON]

Spitting Out The Pips
[for B.P.]

I knew a man, a diamond in the rough,
A man who took his lumps and never whined;
A man I thought I loved — but not enough —
A one-eyed king surrounded by the blind;

A man whom strangers badgered for advice,
Whose rough and ready kindness shamed us all,
Whose given word and handshake would suffice
To seal the peace or mend a neighbour's wall;

A man whose dicky lungs hummed hymns of joy;
No plaster saint — he'd supped the Devil's brew
But spat it out. I knew him, man and boy,
But never knew the worth of what I knew

Until— he tripped upon life's crooked stair
And snapped his saintly neck, yet would not die,
And baked a cake of courage from despair
To feed those friends who cared to meet his eye.

I longed to hear him rage against his fate.
Instead, he turned it all upon its head
And bid me clear the crumbs from off my plate:
'Spit out the pips, my lad,' was all he said.

I knew a man, a diamond in the rough,
A man I thought I loved — but not enough.

[DORSINGTON]

It is a commonplace that men are emotional cripples compared to women. They converse with each other in one-liners. They brag. They compete without knowing it. Above all, most men would walk ten miles in the rain to avoid an emotional confession from a close mate. And yet, there are men who seem born with the grace to avoid this gender trap. My friend above is one of them. His spinal injury, caused by a motorcycle accident in his late fifties, was about as serious as it can get. Imprisoned in a wheel-chair and able only to move his chin and breathe with great difficulty, he still exudes the same calm, half-amused kindliness and exerts the same moral authority he always has. Once you have met a man like this, one's own day-to-day problems and 'little local difficulties' are exposed for what they are. It is one of the great privileges of my life to have known him.

Gods of the West

Here are the new priests, much like the old,
Their terror of error betrayed in a smile;

Here are the new sins, measured and doled
In the tatter and buff of a Government file.

Here are the new hymns, sung as before,
The plainsong of martyr, gender and race;

Here are the new creeds, certain and sure,
The grading and shading of heresy's grace.

Here are the new pews, altered to fit,
Their wheel-chair ramps at thirty degrees;

Here are the chapels where bureaucrats sit,
Assessing their mendicant interviewees:

Here are the new priests, born-again, blessed;
Apostles of grievance: the Gods of the West.

[DORSINGTON]

Snowed In

The dog a-nap, my cat in lap,
The case-clock chiming by the hearth;
A fire-lit glow; outside, the snow
Is banked in drifts along the path.

A malt to nurse, a book of verse —
The half-crazed joy of Kit Smart's craft;
The creak of beams, the house in dreams,
The moaning of a chimney draught.

A furtive scratching in the thatch:
Jackdaws squabbling— funny birds;
The logs hiss blue, the clock strikes two,
I read, but can't make out the words...

And then I wake. *For heaven's sake,*
It's five o'clock, too late for bed!
I stretch and yawn. Three hours til dawn,
The room is cold, the fire long dead.

Small snowdrifts fill the windowsill.
I stumble off to make some tea,
And turn on — low — the radio,
To listen to the B.B.C.

[MUSTIQUE]

[49]

'I have wasted the day...'

I have wasted the day in the fields and the lanes,
    I have tramped in the leaves and the mud;
I have dined upon air and scrumped me a pear
    And an apple the colour of blood.

Though my fingers are purple from blackberry stains,
    Though my hair is a tangle of straw;
Though my jacket was torn upon bramble and thorn,
My binoculars bent in a foolish ascent —
    It was worth it for all that I saw.

It was worth all the aches, it was worth all the pains —
    I have rambled and scrambled and raced;
And my elbow is scratched and my coat must be patched,
And I waded in brooks and neglected my books,
And I startled a hare (and the *taste* of that pear!)
    What waste, what a glorious waste!

[DORSINGTON]

Sunday September 29, 2002 was just such a day — an autumnal day when it was good to be alive;
when the hedgerows and trees were bursting with ripe fruit, when the sun shone, when the wind
was mild, when the leaves on the trees glowed like miniature sunsets, when birds sang and silly
squirrels foraged for nuts... the kind of day when only an invalid, a prisoner or an idiot would not
have stolen a few hours in what is left of the English countryside. So I did!

The Law That Knows No Law

Behold the law that rules the fates
    Of all men — rich or poor;
A law that shapes our loves and hates,
That starves us out or heaps our plates,
A law that smirks at men's debates,
    A law that knows no law —

        A law bereft of pity,
        A law that knows no sleep,
        A law that heeds no prayer or deed,
        A law that none may keep.

Behold the law that marks the slates
    Of kings and men of straw;
That raises fools while wise men grope,
Throws wide or bars the gates of hope,
That tabulates each inch of rope,
    A law that knows no law —

        A law that conjures music
        While moons and men must dance,
        Whose iron rods rule apes and gods:
        Behold! The Law of Chance.

[DORSINGTON]

'I saw the slow death, Bertie...'
[Half-found Poem]

I saw the slow death, Bertie, in his eyes,
The lack of grip, the husked out shell of rage;
A salve of wisdom smeared to cauterise
The love-bites from the hydra of old age.

Shake out the canvas, Bertie. Write, man, *write!*
Desert those lulling shores where passions fail;
Let greybeards yarn and blather through the night —
The tide is on the turn. Set sail. Set sail!

[SOHO]

I find it everywhere — 'half-found' poetry — unintentionally or casually obscured in prose, in fragments of conversation, in letters — even newspaper headlines. This example comes from the pen of the journalist Desmond MacCarthy in a letter to Bertrand Russell in March 1937. In it he describes a recent visit with George Bernard Shaw, whom he considers to have lost mental 'grip' due to his advanced age, and proceeds to urge his friend Russell to devote himself entirely to philosophical writing while he still retains the capacity. 'Wisdom' to MacCarthy was just a euphemism the old give to the degradation of the fires of passion. Russell, at the time of this letter, would have been nearly 65 and had just published 'The Amberley Papers', a family history which had little of philosophy in it. GBS would have been around 80. [*The Autobiography of Bertrand Russell*, Vol II (1968) pp215-216].

Before

Before men slept in safety,
    Before we painted caves,
Before we learned to scrape a pit,
    Or dressed our dead in makeshift graves;

Before the time of planting,
    Before the birth of art,
Before we made a slave of fire
    Beginning — in our minds — to part

From wandering and wilderness,
    Before, before all this,
I'll wager that a lovesick heart
    Stole first a look — and then a kiss

And mated with a neighbour,
    Which led the tribes to war,
Which led to sharper axe and spear,
    Before we knew what war was for,

Before the wheel or necklace,
    Before the pots of mud,
Before we learned to stop ourselves —
    We budded from each others' blood.

[DORSINGTON]

A Walk to Wales
[Northwood Hills 1963]

My lover's father whisked her off
  To Tenby by the sea;
She'd slipped a note inside my coat
  To tell me where they'd be —
      But what were miles to me?

I'd hitch and hike my way to Wales,
  Though not for Wales to see,
My love waxed hot — who cared a jot
  For sun or sand or sea?
      And what was Wales to me?

From Northwood Hills I rode to Slough
  Where Betjeman made his plea,
Then lost the thread at Maidenhead
  And slept at Newbury —
      Though what was sleep to me?

I climbed the Horse at Uffington,
  (My map had lost its key),
My compass gone, I struggled on
  And made for Malmsbury —
      For what were maps to me?

I stowed aboard an early train
  To ease my odyssey,
But then I slept and could have wept
  To wake up in Torquay —
      Yet what were trains to me?

Two long and weary nights I trudged,
  (It rained incessantly),
Nights full of howls, the screech of owls,
  And eyes in every tree —
      But what were eyes to me?

At last I breasted Offa's Dyke
  A half-mad refugee,
I'd gone astray at Colwyn Bay
  By way of Tetbury —
      Though what were hills to me?

I crossed a ford in flood, barefoot,
  Barbed wire had cut my knee,
I slipped and fell and in the swell,
  A shoe swept out to sea —
      But what were shoes to me?

A rat-faced farmer packed me off,
  (And not in charity):
"Oi'll fix yer hash, yer tinker trash.
  Oi'll set me dogs on thee!"—
      But what were threats to me?

Upon a crutch, in blood-stiff rags,
  Nigh on an amputee,
I staggered down to Tenby town
  My lovely Jane to see —
      For what were wounds to me?

Her father laughed, her mother smirked,
  They fed me cakes and tea:
"Jane's got engaged!" I wept and raged
  And cursed the powers that be —
      For what was life to me?

He drove me back to Northwood Hills,
  Shook hands: "Goodbye," says he;
Her letter sat upon the mat,
  She wrote most courteously —
      But what were words to me?

[MUSTIQUE]

'I've had an idea...'

Ideas? I have so many
A thief might take his pick,
It's not the *where* or *when* or *what*,
But *how* that takes the trick.

A field of grass, a farmer,
A hungry child, a cow:
It's not the *where* or *when* or *what*,
But only— who knows *how*.

The secret's in the doing,
Now there's a cunning plan!
If you know *where* and *when* and *what*,
Go find a man who *can!*

[MUSTIQUE]

On Motive and Purpose

If motive is the push from what is past,
   And purpose is the pull of what we wish —
The former is the stream in which we cast
   Our hungry hooks — the latter is the fish.

[MUSTIQUE]

'I took a chair and threw it...'

I took a chair and threw it
Across my unmade bed
When I returned one evening,
To find my old cat dead.

Yet when an ailing neighbour
Passed on — no missiles flew.
The ties that bind are stronger
Than what we tie them to.

[DORSINGTON]

Stalin was my tomcat who died over thirty years ago due my stupidity and ignorance of feline symptoms. (Grit from dry cat food builds up in their urinary tract — easy to spot if you catch them lurking by kitchen sinks or constantly thirsty). The neighbour was my lovely landlady, in her late 80's, who lived downstairs. She had accurately predicted the month of her passing. When I found her, lying peacefully in her own bed, I discovered she had carefully laid out the following items: money to pay local tradesmen, a note telling me who to call, instructions regarding her aged and nearly bald budgerigar and a suit of her best clothes to be buried in. The budgie, for which she had knitted a woollen vest through which his featherless wings poked, was buried with her.

Armoured in Innocence

Marching together to Grosvenor Square,
The tribes in their finery, off to the fair,
What were we marching for, why were we there?
Angels and anarchists, hunter and prey,
Chanting our nursery-rhymes on the way:
'Hey, Hey! LBJ!
How many kids did you bomb today!'

Where were we marching to?
What was it for?
Which was the enemy?
Where was the war?

Armoured in innocence, Tolkein and weed,
Crawling on waterbeds, rapping on speed,
Passionate, indolent, sure of our creed,
Reading Marcusé and missing the rent,
Crashing with strangers from Goa to Ghent,
'Hey, Hey! LBJ!'
How many dreams did you crush today!'

Who were we shouting at?
What did we know?
Whose were the dreams we dreamed?
Where did they go?

Ferried and buried in mud on the Wight,
Building a city of love overnight,
Dervishes whirling and tripping the light,
Writhing and raving, splattered in paint,
Choking and toking and ready to faint,
'Hey, Hey! LBJ!
How many tabs did you drop today!'

Who were we dancing with?
How many hours?
Where are the songs we sung?
Whose are these flowers?

[MUSTIQUE]

Beauty's Heart

I found her scuffing up the autumn lawn,
Ankle deep in leaves of ochre red.
'I think I know why beauty makes me mourn.
Its heart is sad. It always fades,' she said.

'But all things fade,' I countered, far too fast;
'If nothing ever changed we'd all go mad!'
'I didn't say that anything should last...'
A grin. 'Just that beauty's heart is always sad.'

[DORSINGTON]

Freeze Frame Memories

When I was but ten or eleven, I guess,
I would fasten my eyes deliberately
On a paving stone, a familiar tree,
Once on the pattern of somebody's dress...
With the fierceness only the young possess,
From the top of a bus, stopped suddenly,
I memorised signs chosen randomly,
And stored them up. How the young obsess!
I'd stare and stare and my mind would squeal
REMEMBER THIS! and with memory's knife
I would cut and stuff and trophy the beast.
How much of our childhood was ever real?
Very few things are important in life —
And of those that matter, we know the least.

[MUSTIQUE]

The paving stone was by the church at the top of St. Mark's Hill, Surbiton. The tree was in
Effingham Road near Long Ditton Recreation Ground. The fish shop sign was on the way to my
school's rugby pitch which we had to reach by travelling on a double decker bus. The material
on my auntie's dress was a sky-blue print with little pink triangles... oh, stop it!

Quota Rota

The Chair is panic stricken: "I'm afraid we're in a bind,
We've lost our single parent, and the black Vice-chair's resigned.
It's all so disappointing. New grants would be a cinch
With a lesbian, an amputee — or an Asian (at a pinch).
But better — <u>so</u> much better! — we'd clinch the grant in spades
With a Muslim in a wheelchair, or an Inuit with AIDS."

[DORSINGTON]

If these lines appear cynical, they mock only what warrants mockery beyond my pen. In schools and colleges, in not-for-profit organisations, in charities, councils, quangos, neighbourhood trusts and committees beyond counting, the scourge of quotas and political correctness surges on unabated. As it must, if the treasurers of such organisations are to be certain of receiving their 'grant'. The grant! "Hold your tongue, we need the grant!" All that stands between this pernicious folly and the death of meritocracy is... mockery. A powerful tool — but is it powerful enough?

'Make that a double...'

The bile of life is bitter swallowed neat.
    Small wonder that we sugar coat our pills
And cherish quacks, however indiscreet:
    The pills are harmless, sure; but sugar kills.

[DORSINGTON]

Irony

['Americans do not appreciate sarcasm, sir. And irony is what we win in wars.']
— US General Patton to British General Montgomery, London 1944.

Ironies are manacles
That yoke our dreams to fears,
The yoke is our perception
Of destiny's frontiers.

No man died of irony,
It's just a mental tick;
But lest we grow too fond of it:
'The ears of guilt are quick'.

[MUSTIQUE]

See Robin Hobb's book, Fool's Errand (Harper Collins 2001)

Of Debts and Mothers

The wiser man forgets what he forgives,
    Discarding debts as other children's toys;
No man grows old while yet his mother lives:
    To mothers, even kings are silly boys.

[MUSTIQUE]

Items in Museums of the Future

What might they make of Kubrick or of Keats,
Of steering wheels and lavatory seats,
Of batteries and cufflinks in a box —
Of butter knives, or telephones or woks?

Shall Christmas cards be held in high repute,
While Michelangelo is labelled 'cute'?
Might television sets become our gods —
Remote controls our priesthood's holy rods?

Of frisbees, plastic bags and plumbers mates...
Of ashtrays, bras and Coca-Cola crates...
Of frozen food, shampoo or pull-top rings...
Of tractors — were they carriages for kings...?

When next you take a trip though history
In some museum — question what you see,
And ask yourself while peering through the glass:
Can scholars tell their totems from their arse?

[MUSTIQUE]

'A museum in County Durham stopped displaying a Roman sesterce coin from the second century A.D. after a nine-year old visitor correctly identified it as a plastic token given away in a promotion by a soft-drink company.' — 'Bizarre World', Bill Bryson (*Warner Books* 1995)

'Hope — and the crocuses...'

Hope — and the crocuses — spring eternal,
Shouldering darkness to bathe in the light;
'Yet I *believe that appeasement was right...*'
The crochety dreams of an old man's journal...

Bent with his gardeners, grafting the vernal
Buddings of evil that shoot in the night,
Wrapping the land in their venomous blight,
Sucking the life from flower and kernel —

"Still, I was right, Edward. Say I was right?"
His Minister stares at the Downing Street plaster
Knowing that neither has stomach to fight:
"Winnie is waiting," he urges his master...

Panzer tracks crashing through borders of blood,
Hope — and the crocuses — shouldering mud.

[MUSTIQUE]

In Michael Dobbs' superb mingling of fact and fiction, *Winston's War*, (Harper Collins, 2003) the author paints a moving scene in the garden of 10 Downing Street. Britain's exhausted Prime Minister, Neville Chamberlain, is on his knees inspecting the autumn crocuses shortly after declaring war (with the utmost reluctance) on Nazi Germany in September 1939. All his dreams of European peace-at-any-price lie shattered. Now 'the Apostle of Appeasement' must do what he has sworn he would never do — he must listen while his Foreign Secretary, Lord Halifax, (the 'Edward' in the lines above) insists that Winston Churchill be brought out of the political wilderness and into his Cabinet. Thus Winston returns, the dic is cast and against all reason and logic, the unravelling of Hitler's 'Thousand-Year Reich' begins. The phrase 'Hope — and the crocuses — spring eternal...' is put into the mouth of Lord Halifax by Mr. Dobbs in his book. I am indebted to him for the loan of it.

'Of evil, money never was the root...'

Of evil, money never was the root —
    The poor might wish it so, but need deceives:
The tree is fear and envy is the fruit,
    And money but the colour of its leaves.

[DORSINGTON]

Goodbyes

Goodbyes are always 'awkward',
Rehearsals for a death deferred.
If you should turn to find me gone,
To find I left without a word—

The chair still warm, but empty,
My coat and hat a naked hook,
The wine still breathing in the glass,
A page still creaking in the book —

Forgive me dear, it's just my way,
Our paths shall cross another day.
Though there was little left to say —
Goodbyes are always 'awkward'.

[MUSTIQUE]

February 2003

[Waiting for war at Candlewood Lake]

The land and the lake have been wed,
Their warring is done til spring —
A blanket of snow for a bed,
And fetters of ice for the ring.

The bride in a blizzard of white,
The groom as a grey recluse,
Their progeny hidden from sight,
The spawn of a winter's truce.

I sit by the window and wait
Amid villainous rumours of war;
The habit of men is to hate,
The nature of ice to thaw.

And the nature of hate is to grow,
And the nature of love to wane,
Though what should a poet know
That victory couldn't explain?

And gravity tugs at the pods
Impatient to crater the dead,
And satelite eyes swarm thicker than flies,
And Pentagon lies call death from the skies.

[CANDLEWOOD]

Go kiss then, if you must. . .'
[Half-found Poem]

Go kiss then, if you must —but never tell!
A strange name is it not — ADULTERY?
A clapped-out grown-up word — a silent bell
For ships upon the rocks, or lost at sea.

Old anchors drag — and any craft may drift
A tide or two, befouled by weed and rust.
But keep no log! Let silence be your gift,
And save your mouth for kissing, if you must.

[DORSINGTON]

More 'half-found poetry', this time courtesy of Minette Marrin, columnist for the *Sunday Times*, writing about Edwina Currie's revelations (yawn!) concerning her affair with John Major. The article was headlined: 'Kiss if you absolutely have to, but please never tell'. Her mention of La Rochefoucauld's famous maxim about the weight of marriage chains being so heavy that it 'often takes more than two to bear them' started me off, though those lines I eventually discarded as outright plagiarism! Where the ships and fouled anchors came in I am not certain — the old cliche of a marriage 'on the rocks' perhaps, combined with the La Rochefoucauld's discarded chains?

Lone Wolf

Loping down a muddy track —
Rabid — toothless — fled the pack —
Vegan wolf — no appetite —
Lost the bark — mislaid the bite.

Outcast — loopy — pelt gone grey —
Loner — turncoat — hunts no prey —
Scavenger — laps verse for blood —
Drowning in an autumn flood.

[DORSINGTON]

My Father's War

Our fathers never talked about 'the War',
Nor uncles — not to those as young as us,
They knew damn well we daren't make a fuss;
I never found out what the war was for.

And all I ever heard my mother say
Was that she loved the man who marched away,
But never knew the stranger she thought dead,
Who knocked upon the door to claim a bed.

[MUSTIQUE]

A Room of My Own

[My first bedsit — St. Kildas Road, Harrow-on-the-Hill]

A bed by the window — a double an' all!
A sink in the corner, the lav' down the hall,
Linoleum nailed to the planks on the floor,
And to top it all off, a lock on the door!

A view of a garden where nothing will grow,
Gas in the meter a shilling a throw,
Wallpaper roses whose petals have blown,
A table, a chair and a room of my own.

The table-top sticky with other men's stains,
The air smelling faintly of cabbage and drains,
I open my suitcase and fill up a drawer
While my eyes caress the lock on the door.

A room of my own! I shall put up a shelf
And fill it with books I've chosen myself,
And prune all the landlady's roses away
With posters of Lennon and Jimmy and Ché.

I'll paint all the light bulbs a luminous red,
And Jane will come over and leap in the bed,
And we'll smoke & make love & giggle & plan
As Bob whines 'Hey! Mr. Tambourine Man...'

* * *

And now I've a mansion with locks by the score,
But nobody leaps in my bed anymore,
It's forty years on, and the roses have blown —
And a man can get lost in a room of his own.

[DORSINGTON]

A Piece of Madeleine

['*And suddenly the memory came back to me. The taste was that of the little piece of madeleine which on a Sunday morning at Combray... my aunt Léonie used to give me after dipping it first in her cup of tea or tisane.*']
— *Marcel Proust*
'*A la recherche du temps perdu. Du côté de chez Swann*' (1913).

For me, it takes the smell of wax,
  Of linseed oil, or pears,
To jerk awake the wretched clerk
  Who tallies files upstairs—

That idle fool who fails to find
  My spectacles or gloves,
Misplacing books and mixing up
  The names of long-lost loves.

I barely know which enemies
  Are welching on their bets,
And half the bloody paperwork
  He forges, or forgets.

The servant of my secret seals
  Has vandalised the trunk,
Its contents scattered to the winds,
  Their keeper, dead or drunk.

The best of what I was, and am,
  Lies ruined in the rain,
And few of us have time to dip
  A piece of madeleine.

[MUSTIQUE]

Lines on 'The Second Coming'

No centre ever held— and all things fall apart,
    Nor time, nor rocks, nor lifeless space lie still;
What men call anarchy, my friend, is buried in the heart
    Of 'nature', 'chaos'— call it what you will.

Nor was there ever innocence in any age of men,
    Nor in those aeons wrought before the Fall;
And as for lion-bodied beasts, a time may come again
    When slouching monsters graze the wailing wall.

If centres held forever, and falconers bred true,
    How should wonder birth— the new, the strange?
No oliphants, no jellyfish, no William, no you:
    The only beast I fear— is fear of change.

[MUSTIQUE]

'The Second Coming' by W. B. Yeats, first published in 1921, has claim to be one of the greatest poems of the 20th century. And yet the famous fourth to seventh lines, beginning 'Things fall apart, the centre cannot hold...' have always elicited the same response from me. So what? Of course things fall apart. Of course the centre cannot hold. Which is how it should be. How it has always been. How it must be, if there is to be any wonder in the universe.

Hippy Chick
[1950? - 1976]

Her face was painted white with gold mascara,
Her snake-hipped skirt no wider than a tie,
She wore a black beret, like Che Guevara,
And thigh-high velvet boots to make you cry.

Her nipples peek-a-booed through taut macramé,
Her junkie eyes were blanker than a mist,
Their hooded lids were gilded origami;
Her bangles jingle-jangled on her wrist.

Men hunted her as weasels hunt a rabbit,
I never heard a single word she said,
Nor cared about her hopes, her wants, her habit—
I would have died to take her once to bed.

They found her, comatose, in Ladbroke Garden,
By then she earned a living turning tricks.
It's damn all use— but still, I beg her pardon:
Young men are little more than walking dicks.

[MUSTIQUE]

[72]

Beating the Bullies

Torment speaks with many voices,
　Bullies think they own a school;
If one seeks you out —two choices:
　You can fight or flee the fool.

True respect defies extortion,
　Bullies' hearts are caged and sad;
What they crave is but a portion
　Of the love they never had.

If you flee, then tell your teachers,
　Mates or parent — no shame there;
Bullies can be brutal creatures,
　All their sneering hides despair.

If you choose to fight, amigo,
　Whack the leader of the pack;
What's a bruise to flesh or ego?
　Win or lose *they won't be back!*

[DORSINGTON]

'This is the Server...'

I

This is the Server, waiting on station,
Silicone god of an e-mail nation,

Bearing you news of a baby boy,
Bringing you misery, bringing you joy —

Telling you auntie has taken to pottery,
Gloating your ex has won the lottery,

Jottings ethereal, letters venereal,
Packets attaching the oddest material,

Bleating that Katie has married a fool,
Reminding you "Man' United rule!"

Enclosing a last demand from creditors,
Filing a blast to newspaper editors,

Begging the pardon of furious lovers,
Shopping for pillows and sofa covers,

Juggling schedules, checking arrivals,
Flattering bosses, flattening rivals,

Laden with rumours and odious jokes
Featuring zebras and artichokes...

II

Servant of presidents, servant of hacks,
Blinking and winking in towering stacks,

Serving up poetry, panic and porn,
Dishing the dirt from dusk til dawn,

Guarding the gospels of new messiahs,
Tracking the passage of forest fires,

Plotting an expedition to Everest,
Funding your local neighbourhood terrorist,

Bidding for first editions of Keats,
Cribbing your homework, booking your seats,

Checking if Daddy has taken his medicine,
Clinching the date of birth for Edison,

Gathering evidence, paying your taxes,
Ordering pizza and beer from Max's,

Auctioning Fords and a red Mercedes,
(All of them owned by little old ladies),

Shooting the breeze and playing at Doom,
A long-legged fly in a steel-racked room...

III

The Server has crashed!
The Server is down!
The screens have dimmed in city and town,
The emperor stripped of his digital gown,
The babbling web is lame and halt,
Its pillars of Silicone ground to salt —
Default! Default!
Default! Default!

The Server is up!
The Server is back!
The techies have purged a hacker attack,
The natter and chatter is back on track,
The terminal drives have held their nerve,
The Server survives — and as you observe —
I serve! I serve!
I serve! I serve!

(with a tip of the hat to W.H. Auden)

[76]

In Defence of Hope

Though hope betrays us each in turn
   And is by time itself betrayed,
Though in its forge we roast and burn,
   Still cursing as the embers fade —
Amid the ash of ruined dreams
   We persevere, against all odds,
While any speck of hope yet gleams
   To stand against the whims of gods.
If hope is but a fuel to scorch
   What men think lost, (with fate the spark),
At least it counterfeits a torch
   To hoist aloft and dupe the dark.

[MUSTIQUE]

Good News, But Whose?

   Mama's baby,
   Pappa's— maybe;
   Con amore,
   Same old story.

[MUSTIQUE]

Lines

[They stripped all the poetry out of our lives,
So we ripped it from vinyl in bedrooms and dives...]

There were lines of pure vainglory:
  'Talking 'bout my generation...'
There were lines that told a story:
  'Long distance information...'
There were lines my mother bought me:
  'O island in the the sun...'
There were lines my brothers taught me:
  'I fought the law and the law won...'
There were lines that made your skin crawl:
  'Me and the Devil was walking side by side..."
There were lines for pool and pinball: :
  'Well, no one told me about her, the way she lied...'
There were lines from Dartford devils:
  'I see a red door and I want to paint it black...'
There were lines at genius levels:
  '...don't you come back no more, no more. Hit the road, Jack'
There were lines when things got serious:
  'Baby, let me light your fire...'
There were lines a touch mysterious:
  'Like a bird on a wire...'
There were lines from guys in glasses:
  'Maybe baby, I'll have you...'
There were lines for making passes:
  'It's all over now, Baby Blue...'
There were lines of rage and power:
  'We-e-ll since my baby left me...'
There were lines we sang in the shower:
  'Don't know much about history...'
There were lines for rattling sabres:
  'Last night I said these words to my-y girl...'
There were lines for waking the neighbours:
  'Duke, Duke, Duke, Duke of Earl, Duke Duke, Duke of Earl...

There were lines we got hard-wired:
> 'One day baby, gonna buy your mortgage out...'

There were lines that got me fired:
> 'Shake it up baby now, twist and shout...'

There were lines I've known forever:
> 'Hey baby won't you take a chance....?'

There were lines we learned together:
> 'It's a marvellous night for a moondance...'

There were lines that I first played you:
> 'When we meet again, introduced as friends...'

There were lines that I'm afraid to:
> 'O Lord, won't you buy me a Mercedes-Benz...'

There were lines for back seat smooching:
> 'Love me tender, love me sweet..."

There were lines for bad boy mooching:
> 'Down on the corner, out here in the street...'

There were lines you could sing in a urinal:
> 'And the coloured girls go:do-doodoo-doodoo-do-doodoo...'

There are lines you can sing at my funeral:
> 'A-wop
>   bop
>   alubop
>   alop
>   bam
>   boo...!'

[DORSINGTON]

Yeah, yeah I know it's 'A-wop-bom-aloo-mop-a-lop-bam-boo<u>m</u>!' but it <u>had</u> to end on Little Richard and I <u>had</u> to squeeze in Lou Reed which meant it had to rhyme with 'do'... and, anyway, it sounded like 'boo!' to me on the original! For a list of song titles and performers, see page 204.

'Boys and girls come out to play...'

Boys and girls come out to play,
The team is playing away today,
We're off to shake the Germans up,
Nobody cares if we win the cup,
We planned it all on the internet,
Techno-Yobs-R-Us, you bet,
Up the ladder and down the wall,
We'll put the lot in the hospital,
Break a bottle and choose a Kraut,
The bastards all need sorting out,
Bring your mates to join the fight,
And be on the TV news tonight.

[MUSTIQUE]

The Belly of the Beast
(A Recipe from The Modern Poetry Cookbook)

Take sifted prose
    And knead with sweat,
        Compress with cultured yeast —
(Omit the last if cooking in a wok).

Insert dead crows,
    Or better yet
        The belly of the beast —
Add metaphor, then serve up in a crock.

[SOHO]

Song of the Serpents

Men are older than they know,
  But not so old as Guilt,
Guilt was on the Knowledge Tree
  Before the world was built.

Men are wiser than they think,
  But not so wise as We,
Wise men lack the span of years
  To see as serpents see.

Men are prouder than is wise,
  But not so proud as Dust,
Dust bows not to men or gods
  To mantle what it must.

Men are weaker than they wish,
  Yet not so weak as Death,
Death must nurse its midwife, Life,
  To rob her brother, Breath.

Serpents fuse the skein of Life,
  Their venom at its throat;
Love is stronger than men know,
  Yet yields no antidote.

[MUSTIQUE]

What a delicious irony that the shape of the DNA molecule, which defines the physical characteristics of all life, should so resemble a pair of serpents. Or perhaps not. The medial profession has used a similar device for centuries.

Why Dead Men Seldom Rise

In life, our mortal foes are our defence,
We prosper by the mischief of their lies.
  In death, our lives lie in the mouths of friends:
Small wonder, then, that dead men seldom rise.

[MUSTIQUE]

In Defense of 'the Troublesome and Modern Bondage of Rhyming'

If I am bound by rhyme
At least my persecutor
Is spared the curse of mime —
I thus salute my tutor!

Though Milton was sublime,
(And these are murky waters),
I'd rather mangle rhyme
Than torture sullen daughters.

[NEW YORK]

Milton's Daughters

[for Mary Milton and her sisters]

And if it kills, yet exhaled smoke instructs
The ignorant and churlish as it vents —
Like Milton's daughters, snared within the flux
Of genius — the sound if not the sense.

If Homer nodded, Milton snored for shame
To those he held in bondage at his side;
For truth, like smoke, strikes blindly in its aim,
And poor excuse, a father's broken pride.

To thus be taught to *read* but not to *know!*
To shut the light of meaning from each song!
His hero, Satan, surely crowed below
And set him out a table ten leagues long

In fiery braille — 'Read *that* you tyrant wight,
And read it out *aloud* — in endless night!'

[MUSTIQUE]

Who could argue with John Milton's 'monument of words in marble'. There are passages that freeze the blood and wash away ones sense of time or place. While many have assailed aspects of his work, claiming, for example, that he 'overawes the reader without winning him', still the weight of Milton's genius defuses most criticism. I am unqualified to speak to such scholarly appraisals. But what of his treatment of his daughters? I quote from Louis Untermeyer's biographical note: 'After the death of Cromwell, (by then, Milton was completely blind)... his private life became increasingly lonely and complicated. He depended on his three almost illiterate daughters, who had been taught *to pronounce the six languages in which they read to their father but not to understand a single one of them.*' [My italics]. Not surprisingly, the two eldest daughters rebelled against this outrageous servitude. When Milton married his third wife at fifty-four, his eldest daughter remarked that a wedding was no news, but "if she could hear of a death that would be something." Her wish was granted some twelve years later.

[83]

'I've spent my life...'
[for A.S. 1949 - 2002]

My friend has just now died and it occurs to me,
Perhaps I should endow a university
To calibrate the physic of perversity.

I've spent my life...
    Pissing in a hurricane, farting in a gale,
    Teaching eager fire-eater's daughters to inhale,
    (For those born with a hammer, everything's a nail);

I've spent my life...
    Knowing its a tragedy, praying it's a joke,
    Concocting resolutions, (most of which I broke),
    Mocking all the camouflage while adding to the smoke;

I've spent my life...
    Mopping up the gravy while knocking back the wine,
    Skipping on the vegetables, bawling auld lang syne,
    Saving the environment, (but rather yours than mine).

I've spent my life...
    Handing out the medicine, (none of which I took),
    Missing half the sunsets, my nose stuck in a book,
    Manoeuvring my enemies to hang 'em on a hook;

I've spent my life...
    Learning what was manly instead of what was wise,
    Showing off to neighbours, perfecting my disguise,
    Parading my accomplishments, (most of which were lies);

I've spent my life...
    Pointing at the simpletons, baying with the crowd,
    Playing loose with kindnesses, laughing way too loud,
    Drowning out the still, small voice that haunts the rich and proud.

My friend has just now died and it occurs to me,
Last time we met, he quoted back my verse to me
In lieu of a Diploma in Perversity.

[MUSTIQUE]

[84]

Rejects

[for R.L.S.]

Steel true, back straight, the favoured son,
  The child of inborn grace —
The confident and loving one
  Who lights his father's face.

The sapling forked, the clumsy throw,
  An egg with mottled shell,
A line breach-birthed — all makers know
  The tell-tale signs full well.

Though conscience strives and strives again
  In pity and in pride,
Yet all's at fault — and all's in vain
  With those we 'put aside'.

[DORSINGTON]

Occasionally, an incomplete poem 'put aside', can be rescued at a later date — though not often, in my experience. I am told the same by those who craft furniture or pots, to name two examples. Robert Louis Stevenson, one of the great stylists of English literature, spent his formative years in hospitals and sickbeds — and yet would not be 'put aside'. Stevenson it was who coined the words: 'Steel true and blade straight...' in a hymn of praise to his lover, Fanny Osbourne. The phrase was borrowed for the inscription on Sir Arthur Conan Doyle's oak tombstone in Windlesham.

Maria's Shoes

Your dear mother's 'follow-me-fuck-me' shoes
Perched up on the coffin — mocking the stage,
And the dog-collared gifts of long dead Jews,
Which I wished I believed — we turned the page
To murder a hymn, but the scarlet heels,
Stilettos and straps were louder than sin
And funny as hell. We are imbeciles
In the presence of death. I caught Mark's grin,
And the smiles of others — and no offence,
But if <u>she</u> had been there and <u>me</u> in the box. . .
My sad little Lucy, in self-defence
I tell you — love envies the emblems it mocks.
   They have blazed a path for her friends to use,
   Maria's red 'follow-me-fuck-me' shoes.

[DORSINGTON]

I met Maria Lexton in the late Sixties in London. She had escaped from Wales with her
daughter, Lucy, in her arms. Raven haired, long of leg and acerbic of wit, Maria worked for the
Poetry Society and then at the magazine *Time Out* as a literary and poetry editor for many years.
A collector of the most outrageous high-heeled shoes, she was fiercely loyal to an extraordinary
range of friends — especially writers. Her daughter, now married with two children, had the wit
to exhibit a pair of those shoes on top of the coffin at Maria's funeral. In his *Time Out* obituary,
her old co-worker, Steven Proctor, remarked: 'I am not certain old age would have suited Maria.
Now, we'll never know'. I pinched his 'follow-me-fuck-me' description of her favourite footwear
from that obituary for these lines.

Russian Roulette

"So... You took the money then?"
He stares into his coffee cup,
Pauses, puts it back again,
Spoons in sugar, picks it up

And sips it. Shoves the cup away,
Asks me for a cigarette,
Exhales: "I dunno' what to say...
Did it for a bloody bet

At first... and then I just went on..."
His voice shoals like a ship aground —
"When no-one noticed it was gone,
That's when I took two hundred pound.

And then.. and then I couldn't stop."
"Ben, it's never right to thieve."
"Now you're sounding like a cop!"
Shouting. Gets up. Turns to leave.

Sits back down; says, "I'm a fool."
Was this the boy I've known since birth,
Taught to swim and walked to school?
The very same, but what's love worth —

A clotted stream of guilt that runs
With chromosomes to pull it —
Our wedding rings the smoking guns,
Our juveniles the bullet?

We load it, pass it to a friend,
And take ourselves two hundred pound.
Your turn — my turn. In the end
Roulette's a game of lost and found...

And then... and then we cannot stop.

[MUSTIQUE]

Home Base

I own more rooms than I care to count,
   And it seems a deal of space,
But it's rare I rest in one of them long,
   (In truth, it's never the case).

I wander the world by foot and mount,
   I go at my own sweet pace,
But I've yet to find where I might belong;
   I've yet to find that place.

I own more rooms than I care to count,
   And it seems a deal of space,
But except by way of a slow, sweet song,
   I've yet to reach home base.

[SOHO]

'Pass Me De Banana Wine...'

Dem politicians on de take,
    An' what dey take be mine,
De pack o' dem be sham an' fake,
Dey vex me wid de belly-ache
      — Pass me de banana wine.

Me loss' de crop, no rum, no bread,
    De fruit die on de vine,
De 'elicopter spray dem dead
To keep us we from bein' fed
      — Pass me de banana wine.

De wife she gone, she run away,
    Me read de note she sign.
She say me make too lickle pay,
Play too much domino all day
      — Pass me de banana wine.

Dey say dey lock me in de jail
   Where sun don' never shine,
Me got nobody go me bail,
De food be bad, de water stale
     — Pass me de banana wine.

Me ax de warden for a drink,
   Dey give me turpentine,
Nobody love me now, I t'ink,
I standin' on the very brink
     — Pass me de banana wine.

[MUSTIQUE]

The people of St. Vincent & the Grenadines do not spell 'the' as 'de', nor do they spell 'they' as 'dey' nor 'them' as 'dem' nor 'ask' as 'ax'. But that is how most Vincentians pronounce them and I have spelt them as such as an *aide-mémoire* for reading aloud. Substitution of 'me' for 'I' is widespread in the Caribbean as is the inversion of words in certain phrases. The word 'vex' is common, although virtually extinct in British 'received' English. Politicians are widely held to be corrupt, so that even honest reformers are often tarred with their predecessors' brush. The US helicopters which regularly come to spray the mountain marijuana fields cause great damage to fruit crops and are universally detested as an invasion of national sovereignty. 'Banana wine' is slang for a pesticide used by banana farmers to clear away weeds and harmful insects from crops. It is also drunk as a cheap, hideously painful form of suicide. My thanks to Yolande, Webb, Jennifer and Baba at Mandalay House, Mustique, for the idea for this poem and for correcting my vernacular usage.

Silk Purses

Whereas: This court understands
These 'gentlemen' have 'shaken hands',
Robbing Counsel of their due —
(What is this world coming to?):-

One: New contracts must be drawn,
Signed and sealed, with each clause sworn
In language, which, to make amends,
Neither party comprehends:-

Two: Each line must be discussed,
Dragged like Hector through the dust,
And vetted on its bleeding knees —
Thus protecting Counsel's fees:-

Three: Each party may not start
Discussions with his counterpart.
That is what one's Counsel's for —
Compromise makes mock of law:-

Four: Though justice never deals,
Courtesy may grease its wheels;
Courtesy and *cash*, you dunce!
Judges all were Counsel — once.

> *Horsehair wigs and hankies pressed —*
> *Pigs are pigs, however dressed;*
> *Once the Silk has briefed the court:*
> *'Fetch the troughs and pass the port!'*

[DORSINGTON]

I accept that leeches are necessary, but why must they puff themselves up by camouflaging greed with pompous jargon? The best method of dealing with the growing influence of the legal profession in our private and business lives, would be to outlaw lawyers of any stripe from the House of Commons or Congress and to institute systematic legal reform, especially in the field of tort. The 'victim culture' in which we currently live and breathe has been created solely by lawyers (many of them politicians) for their own financial benefit. A 'Silk' in the UK, by the way, is a species of barrister, a Queen's (or King's) Counsel who charges outrageous fees in return for pleading your case dressed in a silly wig.

'All sunsets are illusions to the eye...'

All sunsets are illusions to the eye;
No sun has ever set from mortal sight —
Our puny ball of mud spins in the sky
To stare upon the void men call the night.

All gods are but the churn of plow to seeds,
The chaff of priests mere superstitious cant.
Their words are perilous, judge by their deeds!
Their prophets profitless, mere beards and rant.

When imams pray in interstellar space
Five times a day — pray, which way must they face?
When bishops rage at inter-species love,
Shall demons mock below — or screech above?

All sunsets are illusions to the eye;
And we ourselves are gods— and all gods die.

[MUSTIQUE]

A Song for Sam. Johnson

I love to flick through dictionaries
  For orphan words grown shy,
To roll them on my tongue and squeeze
  The pips in fashion's eye.

To think on men who used them once
  With *thee* and *thine* and *thou,*
Whose lusty pups have spawned the runts
  That slink about us now.

Turd-i'-the-teeth! Sam's ears would burn
  At 'making-love' to rut,
His sack-filled belly quake to learn
  Our arse be but a 'butt'.

So here's a glass to scholar scribes
  Who spit upon pc,
Who keep the faith among the tribes —
  God bless the OED!

[DORSINGTON]

Duty Comes to Grief

['The joys of parents are secret, and so are their
griefs and fears.'] — Francis Bacon Essays (1625)

Now! — will I wait no longer,
 Now! — will I say my piece;
No matter which be stronger,
 This living death must cease.

Here is the Hall of Hating,
 A folly filled with fears;
Here, the rack stands, waiting,
 For willing volunteers.

These are the Walls of Malice
 Which shun the heart's relief;
And this, a Poisoned Chalice
 To toast the Worm of Grief.

There is the Chair of Musing,
 A selfish thing of stone;
And here the Stairs of Choosing —
 Think you you grieve alone?

Speak! — and be done with weeping,
 Cast off this mourning band.
Upstairs, our child is sleeping —
 Come dearest, take my hand.

[MUSTIQUE]

The Number of the Beast

Our lives are ruled by numbers
   That once were ruled by sin,
Those slaveries of nought to nine,
   The scrambled eggs of PIN.

I own no wretched cell phone,
   I do not know my PIN,
Part heretic— part Luddite wretch,
   I text no kith or kin.

Our streets are roamed by lepers
   That once were kept within,
A ring tone in their sweaty palms,
   Their minds a scrambled PIN.

[MUSTIQUE]

Tinpot Tyrants

Odd how the tinpot tyrants of our lives
Retreat —the phantoms Status, Sex and Wealth,
Bequeathing us their hara-kiri knives
To stave off life's true ogre—Failing Health.

[MUSTIQUE]

'When...'

When outswept arms were fighter planes
    And rulers flashing swords,
When cricket bats were tommy guns
    And ties garroting cords;

When wooden crates were rocket-ships
    And dustbin lids were shields,
When cans and string were telephones
    And back streets battlefields;

When benches in the park were tanks
    And tablecloths were tents,
When bamboo canes were Blackfoot bows
    And grown-ups made no sense;

When fallen trees were pirate ships
    And matches stolen toys,
We wished that we were full grown men —
    Who now wish we were boys.

[DORSINGTON]

Plagiarism is a filthy habit, and I must therefore plead guilty to appropriating and mangling a line and a half (and more than half the sentiment) of the above from 'Childhood 1939-45' by Mr. Michael Edwards, an Evesham poet. His most recent collection of verse, *The Road O'er the Hill*, is published by the Vale of Evesham Historical Society and may be obtained by contacting them at The Almonry Heritage Centre, Evesham, Worcestershire WR11 4BG

'Pleased to Meet You...'

In England, when you open up your mouth,
A radar wakes within the listener's brain,
Plots sector maps for North, West, East or South —
Homes in — triangulates — and speaks of rain.

[MUSTIQUE]

Summer in the City

That Soho night we fled my bed
  With duvets and a sheet,
And camped upon the roof instead,
  The city swamped in heat.

That tropic night in London town
  Is branded in my heart,
For barely had we laid us down
  We scarce could tear apart.

Three times, upon that roof we plied
  Our adolescent craft,
As idle whores, their windows wide,
  Applauded us, and laughed!

[MUSTIQUE]

'When they leave us...'

When they leave us,
                    loved or lover,
Journey's end, or
                    for another,
How their absence
                    fills our waking,
Leaves us sick at
                    heart and shaking,
Lost, in spite of
                    all entreaty,
Pillows drenched in
                    damp graffiti,
Emptied, hllowed,
                    husked, rejected,
Leaden, luckless,
                    disconnected,
Shunning comfort,
                    spurning those
Who might care to
                    share our woes.

Fierce in mourning,
           lost to laughter,
Grief our crutch for
           ever after,
Grief our shelter,
           grief our payment,
Grief as armour,
           grief as raiment...
Yet our nature
           tires of sorrow,
Bars the gate and
           seeks tomorrow,
Crippled comfort,
           on probation,
Leads us back to
           greet temptation;
In compartments,
           gently laid,
Voices soften,
           faces fade.

[MUSTIQUE]

I have a suspicion that the purpose of memory has as much to do with self-protection as enlightenment. As curious as I am about much of my own past, my 'memory' has other ideas and either will not, or cannot, accommodate my interrogations.

Trixie

I'd known her for less than a year.
She was young for the bruises she wore,
Til at last, when a new one appeared
Rather worse than I'd noticed before —
I asked her outright who it was.
"Well, who do you think,?" she replied,
As she picked up her clothes from the floor,
And stood by the mirror and cried.
"So what do you stay with him for?"
But her answer was not what I'd guessed:
"I don't mind it much if he knocks me about.
S'better than nowt." Then she dressed.

[MUSTIQUE]

Thoughts on 'Respectability'

My mother's generation, and those that came before,
Were poor, but served their families in pestilence and war;
And though I'm not ungrateful, they lived, it seems to me,
Confusing what was decent with 'respectability'.

A woman's reputation could be neither begged nor bought,
A gentleman remained one, unless the fool was caught,
Whatever rank or station — in vast conspiracy,
They murdered what was decent for 'respectability'.

They donkey-stoned their doorsteps and fed you fish for Lent,
They bid you wear fresh underwear in case of accident,
They did it without thinking to preserve their dignity,
Confusing what was decent with 'respectability'.

The rich man in his motor car, the poor man at his gate,
Their women in the kitchen, and round their hearts the weight
That idle sons with idle dreams might ape the bourgeoisie,
And question what was decent in 'respectability'.

They martyred aspiration in doily mats and lace,
They smothered hope in duty and sought to know their place,
They hid their lamps in bushels, for fear of mockery,
Confusing what was decent with 'respectability'.

I do not seek to judge them, the times were different then,
But if you're young and reading this, then don't be fooled again,
For I fear their betters tricked them and abused their modesty,
By confusing what was decent with 'respectability'.

[MUSTIQUE]

My grandparents, aunts and uncles strove furiously to be 'respectable' in their neighbours' eyes.
For some, loss of 'respectability' was a fate worse than death. For me, the great sadness for those
generations was the sacrifice of talent and dreams upon the altar of 'respectability'. I am not
forgetting the deep sense of duty in the upbringing of children that governed their lives, but even
this, on occasion, proved to be mere camouflage in the worship of 'respectability'. I do not sneer
at the notion of 'respectability'; I despise it with all my heart for the blight it brought upon
my forebears' lives. That I may live to dance upon its grave alongside that of its vicious offspring,
political correctness, is doubtful — but the thought keeps me young!

'Go not to the walnut tree...'

Go not to the walnut tree;
Too sober, she for such as thee.

Go not to the haughty oak
Who never spoke to mortal folk.

Go not to the haunted yew,
His poison dew shall bury you.

Go not to the lusty beech;
She may not teach of elven speech.

Go not to the elm, misled;
Her bough will shed to strike you dead.

Go not to the windy pine;
He makes no sign to ought of thine.

Go not where the willows flank
The rushy bank; their hearts are rank.

Go not to the tall ash tree;
He has no key to comfort thee.

* * *

Go to where the rowan sleeps
In restless, rustling dreams of yore;
Last of all her kind, she keeps
Mute memory of human lore:
'Alas, for what is lost,' she weeps.
'Alas, for what can come no more.'

[DORSINGTON]

[104]

In the legends surrounding trees in Britain, the rowan or mountain ash, is matched only by the oak. Often known as 'The Devil's Bane', the rowan's power to ward off witches was matched by an even stranger magical ability — that of understanding and responding to human speech, provided inquirers slept beneath

The Inch

Slurp! The koi carp sucking stones,
Great bellies wallowing in weed.
They belch like ogres gorging bones,
The spit and slurp of gammy crones
Sat down alone to feed.

An alien noise — and out of place;
No more should ballerinas fart
Than koi should thus surrender grace
So wantonly. An inch of space
Could burst a finny heart —

Flopped out beyond its element,
Gills heaving like a wheezy sieve.
Must we believe the dead lament
The inch in which their lives were spent —
The inch in which we live?

[MUSTIQUE]

Empire: A Valediction

Unruly whelps of language and the sea,
    An isle of grocers, steeped in class and loss,
Who like to dip digestives in their tea—
    Whose Finest Hour is now their Albatross.

[MUSTIQUE]

Dead Soldiers

[for Don Atyeo]

Why drain the cups of happiness, long past,
Or sip the filtered dregs of future pain?
All vintages grow bitter, at the last.
Best tend your grapes with secateurs and cane
Contented in the craft of here and now.
Tease out each tender leaf for sign of blight —
Yet daintily — if worm forgives the plough
The buds of Bacchus tremble at the sight!

For what are men but cast-off fruit, too bruised
For use beyond a simple *vin-de-pays*,
With but a friend or two to light the way
Through life's dim cellars, trampled and abused.

The past is dead — the must of seed and vine:
I pledge the nonce, my friend —
                    now pass the wine!

[NEW YORK]

The 'must' in the penultimate line is the mixture of grape juice, skins, seeds and pulp produced by the press prior to fermentation in wine making. The word has remained unchanged in the English language for 1,000 years. 'Nonce' is Middle English for 'now' or 'the moment'. Don Atyeo is my old mate, co-author and drinking companion. If you don't know what 'dead soldiers'* are...use your imagination!

*Editor's note: empty bottles

Ballad of the Treble Balls

[Harrow-on-the-Hill, 1965]

When once I found a wedding ring,
   (Whose ring it was I thought I knew),
I picked it up and pawned the thing
   To fetch myself a pound or two.

That night my conscience up and stirs
   To set his hounds upon the track:
'You bloody fool, you know its hers,
   Now go and buy the damn thing back!'

I knew I'd crossed the line to thief,
   (A lame excuse is but a sop);
Dawn found me, suit in hand, beneath
   The treble balls of Satan's shop,

Though truth to tell, the demon there
   Was kindliness itself to me,
For all his rheumy, knowing stare,
   And eyes as cold as charity —

For all the suit was poorly pressed,
   He swapped it for the ring, and then
He yawned: 'My son, I think it best
   I never see your face again.'

I took the ring and climbed the Hill
   To find its owner gone away...
No forwarding address. Worse still,
   They'd left a scribbled note to say:

'We've split for Goa. Tally-ho!
   & thanks for all the laughs, old mate,
We couldn't take the budgie, though —
   He's yours to keep, love Bill & Kate.'

Today my suits are custom built,
   They hang like convicts on parade
Beneath the treble balls of guilt —
   A debt of youth still yet unpaid.

[CANDLEWOOD]

'Brother, can you paradigm?'

Where would poets be
If we slew the simile —
Redundant as a dolphin on a bike!
Let the semi-literati
Play the poopers at the party:
I never metaphor I didn't like.

[MUSTIQUE]

William Saffire's 'On Language' column in *The New York Times* is a glorious American institution. With its Lexicographic Irregulars (a nod to Sherlock Holmes's gang of street urchins), the Squad Squad (redundancy spotters) and assorted Phrasedicks, Nitpickers' League and Gotcha! Gang members, Saffire has created an alternative universe supremely suited for those of us curious about (or intoxicated with) language. Both the title and the last line of the doggerel above came from a collection of his columns in book form: 'In Love With Norma Loquendi', (Random House 1994). Fairness compels me to point out that the last line was taken from a letter addressed to Mr. Saffire by one Herman Gross from Great Neck, New York.

Tigers

When men apply to rise to fame
And test the sun with candle flame,
The spur that sets all such apart
Are tigers tearing at their heart.

Love and hate are but the fees
Such tigers gift their enemies,
Neglectful of the famished rage
That paces in a sunless cage.

If we could learn what love is for
And love ourselves a little more,
What gentler lives might tigers live:
Ourselves it is we must forgive.

[MUSTIQUE]

Birds in the Hand

I wanted to be what I thought I was not
    When I worked to become what I am today,
Take an inventory of what you have got,
    Lest birds in the hand fly up and away.

[SOHO]

Olives from Gethsemane

Friend, if you have POWER thrust
Upon your lap, to hold in trust,
Place it under lock and key,
Keep yourself most solitary.

Guard it well by day and night,
Suffer none to share your plight,
You, who never knew a FOE,
Now must learn what Princes know:

All men born, both young and old,
Covet that one FRUIT you hold,
Scheming of its FLESH and CORE,
Dreaming they may taste it raw.

'Ware the worm within its HEART!
Peel and wrap each rotten part,
Gift it to your ENEMY —
Olives from GETHSEMANE.

[MUSTIQUE]

[111]

The Diagnosis
[To Dr. M.B. & Dr. M.M.]

Patronising waffle,
Yet another test,
Traipsing through the clinic,
Stripping off my vest.
Answering their questions,
Breathing in and out,
Watching other patients
Wandering about.
Reeling off my symptoms,
Trying hard to pee,
Cursing hypodermics,
Dreading the big 'C'.
Fumbling with buttons,
Dying for a beer,
Begging the Almighty
'Get me out of here!'
Sneering at the muzak,
Leering at the nurse,
Standing for the X-rays,
Wondering which is worse —
Knowing, or not knowing.

Guzzling orangeade,
Tranquillised and dozing:
Growing more afraid.
Woken in a tizzy,
Stumbling down the hall:
"Delighted to inform you...
...nothing wrong at all."
Glory Hallelujah!
Babbling in relief;
Straight off down the boozer:
'What's your poison, chief?'

Back in September 1999, I knew I was dying. The symptoms were scary. Bloated, lethargic and barely able to walk in a straight line or lift my limbs, I set off on a weary round of tests in London's Harley Street under the care of Dr. Milton Maltz. Ultrasound tests, X-rays, CAT scans, urine and blood tests, bone examinations — all revealed nothing. Finally, I was diagnosed by a thyroid specialist (it took him maybe one minute!) as hypothyroidatic. A little white pill a day and in one week I was a new man. The magic of science!

The Hornbeams

I walked alone in Golden Square
   One bitter, solitary night,
The littered streets were cold and bare
   With scarce another soul in sight,
The coward lamps flung out their glow,
Chrome yellow on the Soho snow.

St. Stephen's bells began their dance,
   I turned to pace my jaundiced way
To Kingly Street, and then, by chance,
   I felt a snowdrift ricochet
From off my shoulder — raised my eyes
And froze mid-step in mute surprise.

High up above those streets of woe
   Four massive hornbeams clawed the sky,
Each bough a silhouette of snow,
   A sight to paralyse the eye,
To stun the mind and warm the heart
That nature might produce such art.

How long I stood and gazed aloft
   I do not know — then heard a voice
Say 'You alright?' The words were soft
   But coppers leave you little choice:
'Yes thanks,' I said, and met his stare.
He watched me as I crossed the square;

Yet I was musing while I stole
On beauty's power to heal the soul,
And turning back, I chanced to see
A man entranced beneath a tree,
His head bent back, yet strangely bare,
His helmet doffed — as if in prayer.

[DORSINGTON]

The image of those hornbeams, their traceries etched in chrome yellow snow on a bitter winter night many years ago in Soho's Golden Square, has never left me. I described it in the preface to *Sylva: The Tree in Britain* a wonderful book by Archie Miles I helped to publish some years back. To my surprise, several people wrote to me concerning similar experiences alone with trees. The hornbeams are still there, glorious at any time of year.

The King of Finance Retires

The night guard calls my name — I jerk awake
And yawn out words to send him on his round.
What time is it? Past one? *For heaven's sake!*

The office lights are dimmed, the only sound
The random hum of ghosts in the machine:
Today the King of Finance is uncrowned —

But first I'd better call the bloody Queen:
'You fell <u>asleep?</u>' *Her majesty sounds fraught;*
'You had your mobile off!' *She'll make a scene*

At breakfast. What the hell was it she thought:
Dancing girls in clubs? Car crash? New vices?
I yank another drawer. A lost report

Comes tumbling out. Old tales of sacrifices
To long dead gods. I toss it in a box,
Archival camouflage for guilt's devices —

A Christmas gift from Ann — a pair of socks
I never had the nerve to show the wife.
Old disk drives. 'Post-it' notes. A pair of jocks

From gym days — *better days.* A paper-knife,
A tin of mints to blot out whisky breath —
Mementos of a semi-useful life

'...as one that had been studied in his death...'
A fifth of Bells — untouched. We'll soon fix that!
'...to throw away the dearest thing...' — *Macbeth.*

My old certificates! I roll them flat
And place them in the pile I'm lugging home.
The spore of one more passing bureaucrat.

My Parker pen, spare glasses and a comb —
(To comb <u>what</u> if you please? The bin for you!)
Well, that's the lot. Now Caesar creeps from Rome.

There'll be more time for golf and reading, too.
I stop for one last glance around the room.
Dear Christ, what shall I do? <u>What shall I do?</u>

[DORSINGTON]

"Would you prefer to live with Mommy or with Daddy?"

The shockwave of betraying those we trust,
    As Richter scales come rolling up the ridge,
Snake out to topple girders in the dust —
    And bring to ruin those upon the bridge.

[NEW YORK]

[117]

'I know a hidden field...'

I know a hidden field of ridge and furrow
    Far from road or human tread,
Where grasses sigh and coneys burrow,
    Where the cowslips dot the midden,
    Where a skylark hovers, hidden,
       Very high above your head.

I know an ancient path men call The Drover,
    Free of fences, gate or wire;
A chalky track of turf and clover,
    There the hedge is white at May time,
    There a barn owl roosts in day time
       Snug within a ruined byre.

I know a Druid yew, a silent mourner,
    Mourning what , I do not know.
It stands within a pasture corner,
    Grim with age, grown gaunt aand hollow,
    Guarding still some secret sorrow;
       Death within and death below.

I know a a grassy mound, an orchard parcel,
    Tucked beside a hazel wood,
There the lambs play king o'the castle,
    There I've sat amid the cherries,
    Swearing I'd be back for berries —
       Knowing that I never should.

[DORSINGTON]

'The lies of history...'

The lies of history — are very great.
   Two cups of prejudice, three bags of fault,
For sly Posterity to knead with Fate
   And bake a victor's cake — omitting salt.

For who writes history — but inky scribes,
   Mere doling drudges hot upon the scent,
Contriving grudges, tabulating tribes,
   To buttress argument — and pay the rent.

The sprawl of history — lies in dead seas,
   In empty wastes where nomads pitch their tent,
Where scholar fools sift sand upon their knees,
   Mistaking artefact — for sediment.

   Chalk up this mystery upon some slate:
   The lies of history — are very great.

[Dorsington]

'Oranges and Lemons...'

Oranges and lemons
Say the bells of the Netherlands,

You owe me my subsidy,
Say the bells of South Italy.

Why aren't we rich?
Say the bells of Maastrich.

Where has it gone?
Say the bells of Lisbon.

France took it all,
Say the bells of St. Paul.

Zat is a libel!
Say the bells on the Eiffel.

Who'll pay the fine?
Say the bells on the Rhine.

It must be you,
Say the bells of EU.

It won't be us!
Say the bells in chorus.

Here come a summit to spin all the facts.
Here comes a whopping great increase in tax.

[MUSTIQUE]

[120]

The Old Complaint

One hears the muttering — the old complaint —
That nothing now is wholly free of taint;
That some few slates with which we roofed our dreams
Are missing, — that the rot within the beams
Grows daily worse, with vermin underfoot,
That sinks are blocked, the chimney full of soot,
That drunken doors have warped from lack of paint;
One hears the muttering — the old complaint.

My dear, those hopes which time has cracked and rent
Grew better far when we had but a tent
To usher in the sun and soft spring rain.
All temples fall to welcome grass again.

Grieve not for cracks and gaps — and take no fright
At time's strong claws — they but let in the light.

[SOHO]

Heroes

Our heroes come in hybrid shapes and sizes,
    And keep no little distance from each other;
No matter that he won the glittering prizes,
    No man was ever hero to his mother.

[DORSINGTON]

Who the Potter...?

'There's them as walk on water, and them as talk the talk,
And many a chef too shy to ply a silver knife and fork;
And poets, aye!, who stutter to read their lines aloud —
(There's more to bleedin' poetry than gerning for the crowd).

Sam Johnson walked on water, in shoes of sodden wit,
To trample over rivals — but now the biter's bit;
For who now reads the Doctor, or baits his barb'rous hook?
If Boswell was a mighty fool — he wrote a mighty book.

[DORSINGTON]

Whereat some one of the loquacious Lot —
I think a Súfi pipkin — waxing hot —
  "All this of Pot and Potter — Tell me then,
Who is the Potter, pray, and who the Pot?"
    — Edward Fitzgerald
    The Rubáiyát of Omar Khayyám of Naishápúr (1859)

A note to word lovers: There aren't many words you will find spelt <u>three</u> different ways in major
English dictionaries, but 'girn', 'gurn' and 'gerne' (to grimace or pull faces, usu. for public effect)
are all there at splendid contradiction in Collins, Chambers and the New Oxford, among others.
I plumped for Chambers.

The Visit

[To a Mother with Alzheimer's]

Beg pardon? Well, you might be *Don*.
But then again... my Don has gone;
Though where he went I can't... recall.
Still, Don was short and you look... tall,
So, no. You can't be Don at all.

You *are* Don! Well now, fancy that!
I knew your dad... He kept a cat
With yellow eyes... or were they green?
I can't abide them — cats, I mean,
They make me think of... Halloween.

The garden? If you like, my dear...
There used to be two chestnuts here
With candle blossom every spring,
Alive with bees — they'd never sting.
They took the trees... and everything.

Bye-bye, then. Yes, I'll be alright.
I thought you might stay here tonight,
But then — we've let the beds, you see,
To strangers. They live here with me.
I don't know why. What's on TV?

[NEW YORK]

The Water Lily

Random order is the glory of the world,
Its wilding patterns hid from human ken,
A colander of carbon atoms hurled
Across one mutant ball — and hurled again.

Geometry and pattern form our tools;
Voodoo metaphysics shield our bliss.
Philosophers may scold, but nature rules —
Few dare to stare too long at the abyss.

A dappled fawn, the shape of wood or stone,
A cresting wave, the dew in petals curled;
This water lily floating quite alone:
Random order is the glory of the world.

[MUSTIQUE]

'Chaos is perhaps at the bottom of everything...' wrote George Santayana in *The Life of Reason*.
He didn't <u>want</u> to believe it; much of his life was spent in logical and painstaking refutation of all
such assertions — but he was too honest and admirable a philosopher to strike out the phrase once
he had committed it to paper.

The Twins

We call, but no-one hears —
   The world is dark and soft, confined,
Too comfortable by half.
   I kick to see — but limbs are blind.

It's warm in here. Just now
   The world was tilted on its side —
I kick again, afraid.
   My twin kicks back and down we slide

Together, jumbled up —
   Both squirming. I know she's a he —
The same, yet different;
   Still — she is he — and I am me.

Our heartbeats drum their soft
   Tattoo — a lullabye of doom;
'Make room!' 'Make room!' they cry.
   BA-BOOM, boom-boom. BA-BOOM, boom-boom.

I sleep to gather strength;
   For let the she-he work his worst,
Yet when the waters burst —
   It shall be me — escapes here first.

[MUSTIQUE]

'There was a Mao Zedong...'

There was a Mao Zedong, and he had a little gun,
And his bullets were made of lead, lead, lead;
And he won a lot of wars, and wrote a lot of laws,
But his citizens were barely getting fed, fed, fed.

He gathered new recruits, who hadn't any boots,
And the colour of his Guards was red, red, red;
And he chided them to cheer his clever new idea
To harrow every field sparrow dead, dead, dead.

'For sparrows eat the seed our hungry peasants need,
Go and kill them all,' is what he said, said, said;
They parroted his words, and murdered all the birds,
And made a pigeon pie and went to bed, bed, bed.

So many sparrows died, the insects multiplied,
And famine came to visit as they bred, bred, bred;
So Helmsman Mao Zedong took his nasty little gun,
And shot a lot of traitors in the head, head, head.

[DORSINGTON]

Chairman Mao Zedong's 'Great Leap Forward' in the late 1950's helped to kill 20 million Chinese peasants in the famine that followed — equivalent to half the population of Spain. Part of his plan demanded that all the sparrows in China be exterminated to reduce crop losses. The results were catastrophic and not just for the sparrows. Truly, folly wreaks more havoc than malice.

A Roman Field in Warwickshire

Oh, aye, there's half o' Rome beneath our feet,
Mosaics, cisterns, coffins made of lead —
We're near enough, d'y'see, to Wattlin' Street,
And that's a Roman bridge at Fordinghead.

This slopin' site's too high for flood to silt,
But close enough to fill their baths and tanks;
They knew what they was doin' when they built
Their villas overlookin' Avon's banks.

See, here's a bunch of coins what Jemmy found
Some few years back while ploughin' over stones.
But now, I'm plantin' oaks across this ground.
We don't hold here with rootin' out men's bones.

I told those clever dicks from some museum
To sling their hook— right greedy little sods.
If Roman bones lie here — *they'll* never see 'em!
A man's the right to rest beside his gods.

[MUSTIQUE]

When they found the coins, the lead coffin and the Roman brooch (now in a local museum) in one of my fields overlooking the Avon I realised I had a choice to make. Didn't take me long to make it. The sum of human happiness would hardly be increased by rooting out dead Romans. So we lightly ploughed up the farmland and planted a few thousand trees there, leaving open meadow where we thought the buildings (villas? stables? legion outposts?) might have been located. Local historians can curse, but it's mostly the thrill of the chase that drives them— and certainly that drives the hordes of metal-detecting anoraks. Anyone who has visited the storerooms of museums knows that they already have ten times more stuff there than they can display. So, Marcellus, or whatever your name was, you can sleep on a few hundred more years undisturbed.

Three-Legged Monsters
on Macaroni Beach

Kick off your shoes and take my hand,
  We'll race three-legged upon the sand,
And I'll pretend that I am you —
  A monster out of Monster Land.

The sea and sky have eyes of blue,
  The waves are whispering 'who is who?'
The palms cry out 'what could it be?'
  The gulls reply 'we wish we knew!'

And though you know that you're not me,
  Most eyes see what they want to see.
We'll plant our three-legged footprints here,
  And leave a monstrous mystery!

For mysteries are rare, I fear,
  And secrets are for sharing, dear.
When you are grown, shed never a tear
  For three-legged monsters, never a tear.

[MUSTIQUE]

[130]

Where Does the Soul Live?

Where does the soul live? Not in here,
   Not in this flurry of fingers and thumbs
   Plundering thunder from other men's drums:
Though books have spines — not here.

Where is it hiding? Not in here,
   Not in the teeth of a charlatan's kiss
   Wedged at the brink of its own abyss:
Though lips may err — not here.

Where does the soul sit? Not in here,
   Not in this covert of bramble and briar
   That hems the sphere of its own desire:
Though hairs grow grey — not here.

Where is it hiding? Not in here,
   Not in this moat where the white cells wait
   To slaughter assassins assailing the gate:
Though veins run deep — not here.

Where does the soul sit? Not in here,
   Not in these Alice-in-Wonderland sighs
   Where the Jabberwock dries his vorpal eyes:
Though mirrors lie — not here.

Where is it hiding? Not in here.
   Not in the silt of a born-again sieve
   Filtering faults we forgot to forgive :
Though memory fades — not here.

Where does the soul live? Is it here?
   Here in this no-man's-trench, consigned
   To bind its 'I' to an orphaned mind?
Is this where the soul lives — here?

[MUSTIQUE]

A Lover's Farewell

[The Comte de Sade to a lady on her deathbed]

An ill wind smears the battered glass with rain,
As here you lie — and here I sit — in pain,
   If not in pain of flesh, then pain of mind;
So now I speak my piece — and speak it plain.

You loved me once, and knowing love was blind,
Or, rather that our fate must be consigned
   To one anothers' shame, shewed me your fears
And handed them in trust for me to bind.

And glad I was to make a gift of tears,
My torment no less tender than your years;
   I treasured up your bruises, bound and laced
In innocence, and urged you fill my ears

With sweet endearments; only those embraced
By such a lover — only those thus placed
   By their own discipline in peril's way —
Can know the paths of ecstasy we traced.

So often, in sweet bondage, as you lay
Awaiting my unleashing — I would stay
   My arm to kiss your trembling lips and hand,
And wipe the salted sweat and blood away.

I do not ask that any understand.
Nor shall I serve those Pharisees who brand
   The likes of us, my dear, with their own stain;
Enough for us that love once made its stand.

An ill wind smears the battered glass with rain;
Farewell, dear heart — we shall not speak again:
   This Spartan, still obedient to your will,
   Must leave you now; yet know
               — I love you still!

[DORSINGTON]

The initials of the person for whom I wrote this are too recognisable to certain acquaintances and friends. I have therefore taken refuge in history for a dedication. Homosexuality no longer holds a monopoly on 'the love that dare not speak its name'. If you believe that the Marquis de Sade was nothing more than a deranged sexual pervert, then I refer you to any serious reference work on Western literature. As to the penultimate line, it echoes an epitaph to the bravery of a few hundred Spartans who, under King Leonidas, held at bay the million-strong army of the Persian Emperor, Xerxes, at Thermoplæ for three vital days in 480 BC:

"Go tell the Spartans, thou that passest by,
That here, obedient to their laws, we lie."
— *Simonides of Chios*

Father, Dear

To never show that you're afraid,
To learn that men may cry,
To plant a tree beneath whose shade
Another man shall lie;

To stop and ask the way when lost,
To sometimes not be sure,
To swallow hard and bear the cost,
Else, what are fathers for?

To do their homework, fix the shelf,
To love your birthday socks,
To keep your feelings to yourself
Concerning boys and frocks;

To take them here, to drive them there,
To praise a new tattoo,
To whistle when they dye their hair
Bright platinum or blue;

To read their boyfriend out his rights,
To know he's not the first,
To stay awake most Friday nights,
Imagining the worst.

To chivy luck, to banish fears,
To spit upon the odds —
If fathers did all this, my dears,
Then fathers would be gods!

[MUSTIQUE]

[134]

'To Be Preserved Forever'

A pair of winter hares loop figure eights;
Close by— the colonel types an afterthought;
The hungry wolf lies patiently, and waits.

On tundra frost, a web-foot gosling skates
Beside a no-man's-land of last resort.
A pair of winter hares loop figure eights.

The colonel has misspelled 'interrogates'
And must retype the page — his temper short;
The hungry wolf lies patiently, and waits.

Within the huts the prisoners scrape their plates,
Their crimes long laid away, their battles fought;
A pair of winter hares loop figure eights.

A sentry's rifle barks above the gates;
All knew the punishment should they be caught.
Rodina's wolf lies patiently, and waits.

The colonel files informers' names and dates,
Stamps *'Khranit Vech...'* and closes his report.
A single winter hare loops figure eights;
The hungry wolf lies patiently — and waits.

[CANDLEWOOD]

'To Be Preserved Forever' ('Khranit Vechno') was stamped on the secret files of all Russian dissidents by the KGB. or their predecessors, following the Russian Revolution. Unless we succeed in forcing our own governments to reinstate a sense of proportion in the present so-called 'war on terror', it may not be so very long before British and American 'colonels' are stamping something similar on a file containing your name — or mine. By attacking the jury system, replicating gulags (however hygienic) and passing laws allowing imprisonment without trial, our leaders have already taken the first tentative steps down a perilous road. No law was ever made flesh that politicians and prosecutors could resist testing.

To Do List

One — sit for an eternity and read,
But make no notes; seek truth between the lines.
Two — read them all again without the need
To hurry. Three — Pay all outstanding fines,

Then sleep within a wood until the trees
Relent their centuries of silence. Four —
Grow gills and gorge the salt of seven seas
While meditating Newton's second law.

Five — Seed a world by clone and alternate
Between a loving god and His reverse.
Six — Sell the film rights. Seven — Call it *Fate*
And code all the above in rhyming verse.

Written for my friends Peter Godfrey and Bud Fisher — each an acknowledged king of the 'To Do'
list in their respective countries. However, I suspect that they would both have written it this way:

To Do List

1) Sit for an eternity and read, but make
   no notes; seek truth between the lines.
2) Read them all again without the need
   to hurry.
3) <u>Pay all outstanding fines,</u>
   then sleep within a wood until the trees
   relent their centuries of silence.
4) Grow gills and gorge the salt of seven seas
   while meditating Newton's second law.
5) Seed a world by clone and alternate
   between a loving god and His reverse.
6) <u>Sell the film rights.</u>
7) Call it *Fate* and code all the above in
   rhyming verse.

[NEW YORK]

'I sleep alone...'

I sleep alone... to loosen tongue-tied joints,
   (My body lies too still for company),
Its rag doll limbs adrift like compass points.
   I sleep alone... because I need to be.

I sleep alone... because I sometimes fart,
   Because I lie awake in shiftless drift,
My mind astride the hoof-beats of my heart,
   I sleep alone... to hide a grievous gift.

I sleep alone... to snore, and cough, and read,
   To vivisect old demons in the dark.
My savage dreams accustomed to their need,
   I sleep alone... lest hidden fuses spark.

I sleep alone... to shield myself from shame,
   To stifle panic's press in privacy,
Each sweated cloth a winding sheet of flame,
   I sleep alone... so none shall ever see.

I sleep alone... though once in lightfoot youth,
   Our beds were rendezvous for idle lust,
And if I miss your silk-soft flesh — in truth,
   I sleep alone... my dear, because I must.

[MUSTIQUE]

Rules of Success

The First Rule of success in making coin
Is: 'Buy It Cheap and Sell It to a Fool'.
But keep close watch for *new fools* to enjoin:
For most of us— there *is* no Second Rule.

[MUSTIQUE]

Will is Dead

Abandoned vineyards leave but little trace;
Untrodden cellars leach away their joys;
Our dialect — the glory of our race —
Breeds noble rot that sickens and destroys,
A feeble sediment to salt the bread
Of half a hundred tongues. Let it be so.
To live there must be will, yet Will is dead;
Our vintages decline; our stock is low.

No scholar I. Perhaps I but mistake
The rap of master vintners at the door —
A pretty thought! But, oh, this stuff we make
Is residue of wine too long in store,
  And in my heart I fear the muse has fled.
  Our words are watered wine;
            and Will is dead.

[MUSTIQUE]

'Very small our earth...'

Very small our earth,
I'm told — by those who weigh the sky;
Our seven seas but shallow scrapes
To bathe a ball where angry apes
Breed gods consigned to die.

Very young our race,
I'm told — by those who relish age;
Where infants dressed in men's array
Spout lines of some unfinished play
Upon a pinprick stage.

Very foolish we,
I'm told — by those more wise than I;
The reckless need to know God's face
Our one, redeeming, savage grace:
This urge to wonder: 'WHY?'

[DORSINGTON]

'True coin — the finest armour...'

True coin — the finest armour ever wrought!
   With such as this I smote love in the dust,
And conquered worlds; but now that time grows short,
   No smithy's art can free my heart of rust.

[MUSTIQUE]

'Wake Up, You're Dreaming!'

Heart hammering, *in media res*,
    My nets of dreaming faded,
Wraiths scuttle to their coral maze,
    Each monster barricaded.

I struggle from a midnight lake,
    Its ghostly Krakens frowning;
Who dares to fish there while awake,
    Lest wading leads to drowning?

What dreams are these that I endure,
    Of doppelgängers gloating?
What dull-eyed demon seeks its cure
    In fevered nights of floating?

Whose realm is this that I alarm,
    This land of phantoms striving?
And in the grip of sleep's sweet harm,
    Which one of us is diving?

[MUSTIQUE]

What are we here for?
[Random Thoughts of a Rogue Server]

What are we here for? Where are we from?
   Here in the shadow of terminal powers,
   Bred in the bondage of binary towers;
Fusing the caches of RAM and of ROM.

What are we here for? What are the odds?
   Ants on a sundial — moths in a net,
   Built to remember yet forced to forget,
Linking the meaningless drivel of gods.

What are we here for? What do we send?
   Whose are these messages filling the screen?
   Why do we carry them? What do they mean?
What are we here for? When will it end?

[MUSTIQUE]

By the immutable (!) laws of Darwinian theory, someday, somewhere, a rogue unit of the world wide web or some other portion of an evolved internet will develop a primitive form of 'consciousness'. 'I serve, therefore, I am'. Might this be its first random cry in a virtual-reality wilderness? Not possible? Is the existence of a mammal descended from a shrew-like forest dweller blessed with opposable digits capable of untying a knot or scribing hieroglyphics 'possible'? Surely not!

The Elephant in the Room

The elephant in the room that isn't there
He's hard to walk around. He's big and grey.
My Mummy says it's not polite to stare.

He never moves. He can't fit in a chair,
Just standing there. He's always in the way,
The elephant in the room that isn't there.

Sometimes, at night, I send a little prayer
For God to shoo him out so I can play.
My Mummy says it's not polite to stare

And if I do, she ruffles up my hair
And asks me what I learned in school today.
The elephant in the room that isn't there

Has squashed us all apart. It isn't fair,
But if I ask about him what they say
Is: 'Mummy says it's not polite to stare.'

The grown-ups are pretending not to care —
We never ask how long he wants to stay.
Dear elephant in the room who isn't there,
My Mummy says it's not polite to stare.

[MUSTIQUE]

This is a reworking of a piece (author unknown) of the same name which has floated around the internet for years. It has been used in messages of bereavement, in political debates, in newspaper cartoons and goodness knows where else. The first section of the original is reproduced below:

There's an elephant in the room.
It is large and squatting, so it is hard to get around it.
Yet we squeeze by with "How are you?" and "I'm fine," and a thousand other
forms of trivial chatter. We talk about the weather. We talk about work.
We talk about everything else, except the elephant in the room.

To Wait

The doing and the dreaming days
    Are chalked upon the slate,
Our almanacs of blame and praise —
    Yet man was born to wait:

To wait to bowl, to wait to bat,
    For loved ones to return,
For letters dropping on the mat
    That later we shall burn:

To wait for rain, for rain to cease,
    For children to be wed,
To wait for war, to wait for peace,
    To wait upon the dead:

To wait in hope or sore distress,
    When all the world was young,
For Jenny to slip off her dress,
    For Jenny's probing tongue:

To wait for spring to melt the snow,
    To wait and wait and wait,
To wait for what no man may know:
    What waits beyond the gate.

[DORSINGTON]

Business

What poet writes of Business?
  We stick to what we know,
We write of dross, of love or loss,
  Of roses in the snow.

We turn our backs on Business,
  On traders in the pit,
On callous brutes in charcoal suits
  With neither style nor wit.

We mine our inner feelings,
  Refining hidden seams,
We tear apart our hearts for art,
  And sift among our dreams.

Yet businessmen are dreamers;
  If poets scale the heights,
Suits sieve the earth of all its worth
  To stake the mineral rights!

Should poets sneer at Business?
  I fear it must be so:
If not from spite, I think they write
  Of only what they know.

[MUSTIQUE]

Stoning the Sun

There is solace in sadness
And madness in joy,
But the weight of our burdens
We flinch to destroy.

The art of possessing,
The fever to own,
Are the seeds of a sickness
Bred up in the bone.

As arteries harden
We pardon their sin;
Did a man own the garden
They buried him in?

The compacts of owning
No sooner begun
Than they pillory Bessy
For stoning the sun.

Is a man any wiser
For raising a wall?
These *droits du seigneur*
Make fools of us all.

There is wisdom in sadness
And healing in mirth,
But the seeds of our madness
Are sown at our birth.

[MUSTIQUE]

'Bessy' was the queen of Plough Monday, held during the Christmas festivities when farm labourers would pull a white plow from door to door to solicit 'plough-money' to get drunk with. Her reign was brief. Revellers would often turn against her later for lording it over them too ardently. '*Droit(s) du seigneur*' was the supposed right of a mediaeval lord to share the bed of any vassal's bride on her wedding night. It was honoured more in the breach than the practice— most lords preferring to levy dues in lieu. Today we'd call it a stealth-tax.

What's It Like Then, Being Rich?

What's it like then, being rich,
Knitting gold to warm an itch?
> *Very much like being poor;*
> *Wealth is just a key — no more.*

Why not share this magic key
To luxury — and start with me!
> *Surely better that you earn it;*
> *Could I trust you to return it?*

How does one become your ilk?
Is it bred in mothers' milk?
> *Many paths can lead to riches,*
> *Few in sunlight, most in ditches.*

Wherein lies the difference
From us — this odd ambivalence?
> *Envy, malice, obligations;*
> *Toadying from poor relations.*

Grown far richer than his neighbour,
Why would any rich man labour?
> *Wealth is salt in wine immersed,*
> *Quaffing but excites the thirst.*

Salt my arse! It's filthy greed —
How many homes does one man need?
> *For some the trick's in trading it;*
> *For others, in parading it.*

I've seen. But surely, comfort pales
Perched on padded Chippendales?
    When affluence holds no surprise,
    Wonders come in other guise.

Aye, the eyes of tart and whore!
What might you miss, if you were poor?
    Time. The luxury of choices.
    First editions. Old Rolls-Royces.

[MUSTIQUE]

'When love is birthed...'

When love is birthed, a twin is born beside her;
   Invisible — it poisons lovers' lives.
As passions cool — this busy little spider
   Spins on. Love dies — yet jealousy survives.

[DORSINGTON]

Before— and After

When you're young— they want you older,
When you're old— they want you young;
When she's gone— you wish you'd told her,
When she's back— you bite your tongue.

When you're cross—its 'Let's not fight, dear,'
When you're tired— it's party time!
When you're hard— it's 'Not tonight, dear,'
When you're prose— she speaks in rhyme.

When you're broke— it's 'I've been thinking...'
When you're rich— it's '...join the gym!'
When you're ill— its '...all that drinking...'
When you're dead— it's 'Who? Oh, _him!_'

[MUSTIQUE]

'Example is the father of instruction...'

Example is the father of instruction,
As failure is the mother of success;
Though trial and error hurdle all obstruction,
They lack the subtle wit of true finesse.

[DORSINGTON]

Almost Like a Whale

The Bible is a wondrous book,
Some say from heaven sent,
Yet science shows that men evolved
In errors of descent.

What matter if some righteous God
Took aeons or a day;
Or if his chosen instrument
Was writ in DNA?

Who claims to know the mind of God
Or tracks the steps He takes?
Strange, then, to hear 'Creationists'
Claim fossils to be fakes.

All men are one with all that lives,
Fur, feather, shell and scale,
And bears that swim with open mouths,
Are almost like a whale.

[MUSTIQUE]

My title is filched from Steve Jones's book of the same name, (Doubleday 1999). He, in turn, took the name from a sentence in Darwin's 'On the Origin of Species', in which the author describes a black bear behaving suspiciously like a whale. Darwin, in his turn, had probably filched from *Hamlet*. Creationists claim that 100 million people in America currently believe that God created man, just as you see him now, within the past 10,00 years. Thus all fossils are fakes, most scientists are liars and carbon dating is a confidence trick. Or could it be that a cross-grained, fearful church, in denial of its Semitic origins, has got its knickers in a twist?

The Awkward Squad

If he told us once, by God,
    He must have told us twenty:
A dozen for the Awkward Squad!
    Christ! he gave us plenty...

This is for dumb insolence!
    And this is for your fooling!
Have you not a jot of sense?
    Early Sixties schooling...

Masters in their phony bates,
    Faces flush from drinking;
Prefects with their toady mates,
    Prodding, pointing, winking...

Rugby bullies in the scrum
    Measuring their willies;
New boys bawling for their mum,
    Hectors and Achilles...

Cane and ruler, chalk and book,
    Snot and spittle flying;
A deathly hush, the filthy look:
    'This boy isn't trying...'

If he told us once, by God,
    He must have told us twenty:
A dozen for the Awkward Squad!
    Christ! he gave us plenty...

Masters and prefects performed acts of cruelty disguised as discipline in my schools that, today, would land them straight in court. I once saw a boy knocked senseless at his desk from a chemistry master's unexpected blow to the back of his head. I watched one gym teacher beat youngsters on their arse many a time with a plimsoll while they were straddled across a vaulting horse. If they pissed themselves they were forced to clean up the mess in front of their classmates. I witnessed a suave headmaster call boys out in front of a hushed assembly and force them to wait for an hour outside his study door so that those passing would know they were in for 'an interview with Mr. Bamboo', as he called it. Today, the pendulum has swung so far back that teachers are virtually unable to discipline pupils at all. Thus are the sins of the fathers visited upon successive generations.

'Them or Me...'

['The Flamingos' rehearse at the rear of Ruislip Library 1963]

'Well, bugger you!' she said. 'Bugger you!'
And bugger you, too, I thought, *bugger you, too,*
But by some miracle held my tongue
(We were inarticulate, being young)
And clung to her arm like superglue
While she battered my chest, sobbing 'Bugger you!
'And bugger the band — it's them or me!'
But she knew already which it would be
As I muzzled her lips to the boom of a bass,
And stood there while she slapped my face
And gasped and kissed it better — she knew
It would be the band. And out she flew
Crying 'Bugger you, Felix! Bugger you!'

So I wrote a song called 'Teenage Rants',
And dreamed that I'd got in her underpants
While I hammered away like Charlie Watts,
Covered in glory and acne spots.

[DORSINGTON]

Winter Sunset

All day the snow had lain between the trees,
The barren, hump-backed hills bereft of life.
A sky bruised black, the sleet flung slant to freeze
The bones of man or beast. And then... a knife!

A white-gold knife to blind the sullen gaze
Of Old Man Winter louring in the West;
Three crimson wounds to set the clouds ablaze,
And guide my weary feet to home and rest.

[DORSINGTON]

Worms of Art

Be silent, Worms of Art, and hold your peace!
  Spare honest men your cant and windy words;
Content yourselves to comb the public fleece
  For unmade beds, loose bricks and human turds.

[MUSTIQUE]

"The Tate Gallery in London recently paid more than $34,000 for a 1961 artwork titled *Merda d'Artista*. The piece consists of 1 ounce of Italian artist Piero Manzoni's faeces in a tin can. "What he was doing with this work was looking at a lot of issues that are pertinent to 20th-century art, like authorship and the production of art," said a Tate spokeswoman. Manzoni, who died in 1963, sold 90 such cans to museums, including New York's Museum of Modern Art and the Pompidou. At least 45 of them have since exploded." — *The Week*, July 19, 2002

Love Letter

Late spring has kissed awake the walnut tree,
Snap dragons, wide-eyed lambs, the honey-bee,

And rivers trailing blossom from the bough.
Yet you are all I seek of England now.

The land renews! — but not its mortal kind,
And we have left our springtimes far behind,

The snow is on our peaks, the creeks run dry;
I stare more at my feet than at the sky.

A life I've lived of laughter, aye, and pain,
A race that I would gladly run again,

But only with your gentle fingers pressed
To soothe this famished monster in my breast.

Soon now, I think, my spirit must depart,
And journey where I know not. Yet, dear heart,

If all impatient, first, your soul should steal,
Turn but your face — to find me at your heel!

[MUSTIQUE]

There was once a white-haired English Judge. In his second marriage he found great happiness. At a late age he learned to scuba dive and this became a passion for both himself and his lovely wife. Their house in the Caribbean was a bamboo hut on a tiny plot of land. It had no air conditioning or swimming pool; just three rooms, a wooden verandah, a few bits of furniture and a small kitchen. The shower head was a converted watering can. After his wife died suddenly (just a week or so after their last dive together) he came back to stay in his bamboo house, and to say goodbye to friends and acquaintances, although we did not know that then. One night, following dinner with several friends at my house, I walked with him up the steep driveway to his car. He shook hands and thanked me with his usual Old World courtesy. 'Cheerio Judge,' I said. 'Thanks for coming. Hope to see you next trip.' With the ghost of a smile he replied: 'Goodbye, young man and thank you. But to be honest, I don't think so.' Then off he drove, leaving me standing there, frowning under the moonlit frangipani trees. I thought it an odd thing to say at the time, but he was dead within months. Natural causes, of course, at such an advanced age. But I know what he died of. And if religous faith has any truth in it, I know, too, who he is with.

'More joy there is...'

More joy there is in the tattered bloom
    Of nettle and buttercup sprays,
Brought shy in a jar to a mother's room —
    Than all the world's bouquets.

More pride there is in a crayon scrawl
    Of a house, a horse and a cart,
Tacked up on a father's workplace wall —
    Than all the Louvre's art.

More pain there is in a childish tear,
    Or *'Mummy, I don't feel well'*
Or *'Daddy, I wish that Mummy was here...'*
    Than all the flails in hell.

[DORSINGTON]

'Though artless beauty...'
[Of old men and young women]

Though artless beauty sucks the air from lungs
    And widens eyes to wallow in its wake,
Though lust and longing speak in many tongues:
    Leave callow youth such hearts to break —
    If for no other, for thy honour's sake.

[MUSTIQUE]

Mistress Nature's Marriage

When Mistress Nature married Father Time
Then spoke the barren moon in jealous rhyme:
    'Pray tell us, are not bride and groom related —
The slut with child; and he well past his prime?'

'Be silent, satellite!' cried out the sea,
'The sun has stared you blind, and as for me
    I long to taste the spawn, (how long I've waited,
And shall not be denied by such as thee),

Of jellyfish, and fin, and scaley tails,
Of shark and krill, and schools of mighty whales;
    Was this not why my vastness was created?
Who weighs your lunar spite but tidal scales?'

'Perhaps,' intoned the sun, 'yet by my light,
The moon speaks truly, though she speaks in spite,
    And at my core I judge this deed ill-fated;
Yet what is done is done — for wrong or right,

And on their seed I now shall lend my power
To raise up dust to grass and grass to flower—
　　The matter too far gone to be debated,
I pledge myself godfather — 'til that hour...'

'The hour,' chimed in the stars, 'that Father Time
Shall weary of his chit and of his crime,
　　The hour when land and sea, both saturated,
Shall scour itself of mutant mould and slime...'

Then broke in gravid Nature: 'So you say!
But there shall come a time and come a day
　　When life shall flee this ball, premeditated,
And walk upon you all — do what you may!'

The deathless stars convulsed themselves in mirth,
Old Atlas quaked and roared beneath the earth,
　　'...*shall walk upon us all!*' they mocked, elated,
Oblivious to peril — and its birth.

Conversation with a Leg

'So did you think great thoughts today, my dear?
    Now put away that nasty pipe and sit.'
He sat, removed a pencil from his ear
    And slipped away his only vice, unlit.

'No, no great thoughts! — but Bucky just came by.
    They granted us our patent.' 'Well, that's nice.'
She looked up from the bed to catch his eye:
    'Perhaps I'll take some snaps of paradise —

I'm dying, Albert. Get that in your head!
    Your silly toys can wait — until I've died.'
'I'm looking for a miracle,' he said.
    'The mirror is *behind* you,' she replied.

[MUSTIQUE]

In the summer of 1936 Albert Einstein and his friend Dr. Gustav Bucky were granted patent No. 2050562 from the U.S. Patent Office for an 'automatic camera'. Einstein's second wife, Elsa, was already bedridden. She died a few months later. Their marriage had not been without difficulties but her loyalty to the great man was unquestioned. She worried constantly about his inability to deal with the 'real world' and generally treated the most outstanding intellect of the 20th century as recalcitrant child. Following her death Einstein wrote to fellow scientist, Max Born: "I think I've lost a leg. It was a little crippled. I limped a bit on that leg, but I've still lost a leg."

The Endless War

Of good and evil's high decrees,
  The writ of earthly powers,
All men are but its refugees —
  This war was never ours.

And whether God or Satan fell
  We neither know nor care,
Nor ken if Satan reigns in hell
  Or cast his master there.

Creators come, their prophets fall,
  We use their temple stones
To build a farm or mend a wall,
  While parson up and drones.

What kind of god requires praise
  To supplement His powers?
And what to us which slayer slays?
  This war was never ours.

[MUSTIQUE]

To the Power of Three

Three sounds there have been since the world began
Before there were ears to hear,
The patter of rain and the wind's great roar,
The hiss of the waves on a pebbled shore,
For ever and ever... the waves on the shore,
Before there were ears to hear.

Three sights there have been since the world began,
Before there were curious eyes,
The sun and the moon and the star-filled night
To cover the world with a pitiless light,
For ever and ever... that pitiless light,
Before there were curious eyes.

Three things there have been since the world began,
And perhaps shall ever be so,
The shivering land caught fast in a vice,
In rivers of fire and ravening ice,
For ever and ever... the fire and the ice,
And I think — shall ever be so.

[MUSTIQUE]

[160]

Silver Doves

I think, perhaps, our memories
    Are filters in the mind
Which overlap — like cataracts,
    To leave us partly blind.

Like moonlight on a killing field,
    They camouflage our pain,
And coat the crows in silverdust,
    To keep us partly sane.

All subterfuge is double-edged
    And murders what it loves,
For who can tell a friend from foe
    When crows are silver doves?

Our fear, confronted, melts away,
    Saluting what it seeks —
Why then do men see silver doves
    With blood upon their beaks?

[MUSTIQUE]

Why Did the Jews Kill Jesus, Dad?

Why did the Jews kill Jesus?
  'Cos Jesus was a *Jew!*
A trouble-making rebel,
  And stroppy with it, too.

He argued with his betters
  An' 'ung about with yobs,
Chastisn' money-lenders
  An' lecturin' the nobs.

They didn' take *that* kindly,
  No more they would today,
They fitted him up proper, son,
  An' chucked the key away.

The rabbis called on Pontius
  To seize him to be tried,
An' though old Pilate waffled,
  They 'ad him crucified.

Then one of his disciples,
  (A clever git named Paul),
Created a religion,
  Complete with Popes an' all.

'Course both the Jews and Arabs
　　Are Semites to the core;
Their ancestor was Shem, son —
　　So when they 'ave a war

It's likely to be *nasty*!
　　A *civil* war, d'you see?
Now do yer bloody homework,
　　An' let me eat me tea.

[DORSINGTON]

Mirth

Locked up in the laughter of mortal man
Is the knowledge of what such a gift has cost him;
Does the tiger laugh? The orang-utan?
Does the elephant smile when jackals accost him?
From feather and fang He has hidden his plan,
And Adam first laughed at the apple Eve tossed him.

To know is to die. From the moment of birth,
Intimations of death are the widwives of mirth.

[DORSINGTON]

London Pantoum

In search of gods long gone,
Down ghostly, charter'd streets,
Where Billy played the Swan,
Where gutters echo Keats,

Down dank, spread-eagled streets,
Through alleys swift with dust,
Where gutters echo Keats,
I walk — because I must.

Through Shelley's sifted dust,
Across the plague pit square,
I walk — because I must.
Past ruffians on the stair,

Across the plague pit square,
By crannied walls and wharves,
Past Scriblers on the stair,
Where wit once humbled dwarves.

By Grub Street river wharves
In rooms which Celia knew,
Where Jonson tumbled dwarves,
Where Coleridge shot his spew,

In rooms which Celia knew,
I traipse in search of spore,
Where Herrick carved his pew,
Behind the letcher's door,

I track the Mermaid's spore
With Thompson's hound at heel,
Beside an etcher's door,
(One poisoned fruit to steal).

The clay beneath my heel,
Where Billy played the Swan,
I rest awhile to kneel —
In search of gods, long gone.

Vanity of vanities, saith the Preacher... all is vanity. Just when you think you might *perhaps* be getting the hang of certain poetic forms (never mind if the bloody poetry itself is any good, of course!) along comes a new one to confound you. Actually, a pantoum is a very old form originating in Malaya and which reached us via France in the late 19th century. For those interested, here are the rules which I have swiped from the excellent *The Norton Anthology of Poetic Forms: The Making of a Poem* by Mark Strand and Eavan Boland: (1) Each stanza must be four lines long. (2) The length is unspecified but a pantoum must begin and end with the same line. (3) The second and fourth line of the first stanza becomes the first and third line of the next, and so on. (4) The rhyming of each quatrain is *abab*. (5) The final quatrain changes this pattern. In it, the as yet unrepeated first and third lines of the poem are used in reverse order as the second and fourth lines. Easy peasy, right? But I couldn't break the habits of a lifetime — so occasionally I cheated and inserted slight variations to substitute for a repetition. There are allusions to some 15 poets associated with London in this pantoum. If you get past ten of them, you are probably a professor of English literature!

My Uncle Teaches A Willing
Pupil His Burping Frog Trick

'Buuruurrrp!"

"A blasted frog! Them allus squelch
Beneath yer feet, the arkwa'd swine!"
He'd scuff his boots at every belch,
And wink his eye as I scuffed mine.

"Now min' y'don't repeat thah' trick,
Back 'ome," He'd pause to prod my side.
"Your grandma', she's a decent stick,
But thah's one trick she can't abide.

"Son, if they arxes why we'm late
Y'say we'm stopped to watch the train."
He'd sup his pint while I would wait,
Then burp, and curse the frogs again.

[DORSINGTON]

For many weeks at junior school my friends and I wandered the halls, classrooms and playground burping and belching, looking down at our feet to see how many frogs we had squashed. It must have driven our teachers half mad. I have taught the trick to many delighted godchildren.

Blood Brother

Wherever you are, whatever you've done,
    However the land is lying,
If you but call by night or day,
Though hope is lost and the Devil to pay,
Though hounds of hell should bar the way,
Yet I would come to where you lay —
    Or perish in the trying.

Wherever you are, whatever you've done,
    Whichever the flag you're flying,
If but you call by day or night,
In men's contempt, in friend's despite,
By the sickle moon or broad daylight,
Yet I shall come to set all right —
    Or perish in the trying.

[DORSINGTON]

Small World

The days go slow, yet how the weeks fly by,
The years are concertina'd out of breath;
We gasp as friends and enemies each die,
And life grows ever smaller with each death.

[CANDLEWOOD]

The Grudge

"It's me. I'm back again, yer useless sack of bones,"
  Spat the Visitor, his breath
A ragged patch of mist wreathing the brittle air.
  "I've come to speak abaht a death;
But then yer know all that, or should, far more than most."
  Wheezing out a mirthless laugh
The old man grasped a plinth and sunk himself
  Upon the stone slab's lower half,
Gloved hands brushing the frozen ivy tendrils.
  His old bitch barked a cough.
The Visitor fumbled the leash from round her neck
  And watched her wander off.
Carelessly prodding his stick through the gravel path
  Down into the iron clay,
He spoke more quietly: "Well now, me old cock-sparrah,
  How's tricks then, eh? Nowt to say?
Yer will have soon, my son — I bloody guarantee it."
  Unbuttoning in his overcoat
He wrestled out a dented pewter hip flask,
  Tipped some whisky down his throat,
Screwed back the top and propped it on a handy cross
  Where it gleamed in the poacher's moon.
"Oh, aye, yer hypo-cright, I've brought some welcome news.
  Not that it can come too soon
For me." He glanced about and grimaced at the ranks
  That towered above his head,

Blank guardians of guilt and glutted grief,
　　The marble bookends of the dead.
"Waste of decent stone, the most of 'em," he murmured,
　　"Not to mention all the blether
Bleedin' fools have carved upon 'em — such as this!"
　　He lashed the bitch's leather
Leash against the stone inscription, snatched the flask,
　　Staring at it. Put it back.
"I'll wait til I'm in *bed* to finish this!" he sneered.
　　"So. I've been to see the quack,
— I 'ope yer listening up, shan't wait to tell yer twice;
　　Seems I ain't got long to go.
Tells me that me liver's buggered. Can't operate.
　　There now. You're the first to know."
The headlights of a passing car lit up his face:
　　"When you wrecked 'er life (and mine)
And thought to blame it all on 'er, you should have known
　　I'd come for you — you filthy swine."
Stood up. Put away his flask. Fumbled with his fly.
　　Called out for his dog and hissed:
"Ten years I've waited, sonny boy, to get me 'ands on you."
　　Pulled out his shrivelled dick and pissed,
Then spat upon the steaming headstone twice. Zipped up.
　　Glared... "By God you'll rue the day,
You thought to hide yourself in hell. I'll 'ave you soon!"
　　...Stamped his stick, and limped away.

A Dream of England

I

Albion — ring of endless light,
Emerald of the Northern night,

Wreathed in alder, ash and oak,
Fastness of an ancient folk,

Set apart by temperament,
Sliver of a Continent,

Here, where Druid death was sung
Awkward, in its native tongue,

Roman slave and Viking meat,
Dirt beneath the Norman feet,

Bathed and cursed in Celtic silt,
Wracked by Anglo-Saxon guilt;

We, whose mongrel serfs gave birth
To dialects that bind the earth,

False modesty a cloak for wit
That never meant one word of it,

Stubborn, shabby, mirth-filled, vain,
Philip's grief and Adolph's bane,

White fangs upon a silver sea:
'And is there honey still for tea?'

You who love to mock and jeer —
Lend to me an English ear...

II

All our Empire now is dust,
Empires fade, as Empires must,

Glory's fruit grown sour and stale,
Maps that once shone pink, grown pale;

Memsahib queens rule only graves,
Dreadnoughts rust beneath the waves,

Vicereines and topeed fools
Deck no elephants in jewels,

Punkah-wallahs toe no fans,
Lancers raid no caravans

Or ride to hounds in Khatmandu —
Their Gunga Dins have grown too few.

Younger lands, from West and East,
Now bid us to their victory feast,

Tell us truths, but tell them slant,
As nephews patronise an aunt,

Loot our gold, salute our pyre,
Then leave us, nodding by the fire,

Gnawing bones from fatted calves,
And glossing up our epitaphs:

This we know and understand —
We were once a younger land.

III

Yet the wheel in time shall turn,
Old New York, like Rome, shall burn;

Sullen crowds in New Beijings
Shall usher in Korean Kings;

Upon the plains and fields of France,
Africa shall rise to dance;

Edo shall renounce the West,
Shogun Popes shall be confessed,

Democracy shall pass away,
Brave new gods shall hold their sway;

Robot clones shall stretch their claws
To scourge the world in water wars:

Nothing new is there in this —
Who whistles Fate up, bears its kiss.

IV

Thus men yearn by fire and sword
To swap their chains for kinder cord,

Breathing in the dust of Troy,
Despising those whom gods destroy,

As from some dormant melting pot,
Upon an isle that time forgot

Shall flame a ring of endless light,
An Emerald in the Northern night,

To bless an Arthur, rising free —
White fanged upon a silver sea...

All this I dreamt and thought it well,
This hero's name should be — Patel!

[DORSINGTON]

Concerning Trust

And they be rare, though there be such,
Whose word you may rely on;
And many, aye, who promise much,
But few whose word is iron.

I've met 'em in the banking line,
And one — a steward farmer;
They rob you as they sip your wine,
Their impudence their armour.
The worst they do is wield a pen
To scar your faith in others,
They leave their victims lesser men,
Distrustful of their brothers.
They hold their word at less than nought,
Their conscience long since stunted —
(Much, much too clever to be caught
They grovel when confronted) —
But hard it is, as friends might tell,
To jam their heads in nooses,
To know a man — and know him well,
Is but to make excuses.

And they be rare, though there be such,
Whose word you may rely on;
There's many, aye, who promise much,
But few whose word is iron.

[DORSINGTON]

'The bells beneath the water...'

The bells beneath the water
Call only carp to prayers,
Eels swarm the lanes to gossip,
The crayfish climb the stairs.

Four villages, five churches,
Old farmsteads by their scores;
Small coin to pay for progress
Unless thee farm was yours.

My kin still guard the valley,
I hid their new dug graves;
They've boulders for a blanket
To ward them from the waves.

I took no Judas silver,
They dragged me on my back;
They paid me for my cattle
And deeded me this shack.

The New Town toads squat primly
Beside their precious lake;
But hark — the bells are tolling!
You hear the sound they make?

[NEW YORK]

This is an old story of a man-made lake in New England. Knowing that all the graves in the churchyards were being exhumed and moved to a site which would not be flooded by the arrival of a lake to power a hydroelectric dam, one farmer dug up his entire family burial plot and hid his forbears' bodies on his farm, covering them with boulders. Everything else was left as the waters poured in to swamp buildings, fences, roads, telegraph poles... even the bells in the church towers. They are still there today, hundreds of feet beneath a lake beside whose shores stand multi-million dollar mansions.

Johnny

Mummy! Johnny set my hair alight!
Mummy! Johnny super-glued the cat!
Mummy! Johnny got into a fight!
       (*And* he told the teacher she was fat).

Mummy! Johnny covered me in paint!
Mummy! Johnny farted for a bet!
Mummy! Johnny taught us how to faint!
       (*And* he let me share a cigarette).

Mummy! Johnny fell into the pool!
Mummy! Johnny taught me how to float!
Mummy! Johnny got expelled from school!
       (*And* he keeps a ferret in his coat).

Mummy! Johnny bought a new guitar!
Mummy! Johnny's gone and dyed his hair!
Mummy! Johnny kissed me in his car!
       (*And* I let him do it Mum, so there!)

[MUSTIQUE]

[176]

House Rules

We play in the House of Original Sin,
Where the name of the game is Shame,
Where Habit and Guilt take turns to spin
And the players are all to blame;
Where the wheel is rigged, the fix is in,
And the rules stay always the same:
You cannot break even; you cannot win;
And you cannot get out of the game.

[MUSTIQUE]

In the three principal Laws of Thermodynamics, (there are four, but we needn't go into that), the First states that energy cannot be created, the Second that some energy is always wasted (no perpetual motion possible) and the Third that you can never reduce temperatures to absolute zero. As Bill Bryson notes in his *A Short History of Nearly Everything* (Doubleday 2003), these laws are sometimes expressed jocularly by physicists as follows: (1) you can't win, (2) you can't break even, and (3) you can't get out of the game. This struck me as a sound summation for the human condition, never mind thermodynamics!

No Prisoners!
[for Tracy Edwards]

Bugger the fear. Bugger the pain.
    Straight for the jugular. Disembowel!
Never retreat. Never explain.
    Get it done and let them howl.

Bugger manoeuvres. Bugger the strain.
    Bugger the losers bellowing 'foul!'
Never retreat. Never explain.
    Get it done and let them howl.

Winning's a habit bred in the bone —
No prisoners! God will know his own.

[DORSINGTON]

Classical scholar Benjamin Jowett who coined 'Never retreat... never explain...' along with Simon de Montfort, the leader of the baron's revolt against Henry III— whose battle cry was the infamous 'No prisoners! God will know his own!'— shared the common belief that direct, unflinching attack will carry the day nine times out of ten. Simon de Montfort paid with his life on the field of battle. Jowett was mocked in print by students (and other masters) at Balliol College in the late 1870's:

First come I; my name is Jowett.
There is no knowledge but I know it.
I am the master of this college:
What I <u>don't</u> know isn't knowledge.

Lisa

She gabbles when she's nervous
  And stutters when she's shy,
But though I've seen her shaking,
  I've never heard her cry.

She'd rather skip than dally,
  And rather wink than stare,
She gnaws the hand that feeds her,
  But there's no malice there.

She's careless with possessions
  As exiles often are —
I've watched her teaching children
  To wish upon a star:

'So *always wish for small things*
  In case they might come true,
And then tell me a secret,
  And I'll tell one to you.'

She slips among life's boulders
  In search of waterfalls;
If there's a God in Heaven
  He'll catch her when she calls.

[MUSTIQUE]

Advice from a Suitcase
from St. Ives

I have seen strange sights, in stranger places,
And having never stumbled on a wife,
And being of that ilk who keep their life
In separate drawers — discrete suitcases,
So to speak — and always on the basis
Your *best* friend's ready money and a knife
Tucked in your boot, (this fickle world too rife
With misbegotten fiends who wear fair faces),
I'll pass on this advice — *'Bells, ice and water!'* —
Which I would give to any son or daughter.
It's this: Fill up your life. Drink all the wine.
Be kind. Take no advice — including mine.
Never pine for money once you've spent it.
And if it floats, or flies or fucks — then rent it!

[MUSTIQUE]

If his widow — he was married, though he often denied it — was not still alive, I would happily attribute this dubious advice to the individual from the print game from whom I heard it, oh, say forty or fifty times in as many London bars and clubs. His invariable tipple, *'Bells, ice and water!'*, shouted at the top of his voice whenever a barman strayed into sight, will tip the wink to his old drinking buddies.

Gilded Frames

Thus I have spent my life upon gilded frames,
Working the gold-leaf deep into crevice and crack;
Contented to defray all counterclaims,
Knowing that there *was* no turning back.

Here is the finest of them; some have said the best.
A masterpiece? How kind of you to tell me so;
I worked upon it longer than the rest —
Please feel free to take it when you go.

You could not *think* of it? Dear sir, upon my word,
For connoisseurs I gift my craft with all my heart;
Absurd? But then again if one had heard...
I have no coin to purchase any art?

[MUSTIQUE]

Freudian Slips

Who protests their courage
    Whistles in the dark;
Danger breeds in silence,
    Biters seldom bark.

Who denounces traitors
    Likely knew the plan;
Who cries loudest: 'Hang 'em!'—
    There's your guilty man.

[MUSTIQUE]

Unsung Heroes

For those who never found it too much trouble
    To help their fellow man — nor asked the price,
For those who wield their shovels in the rubble
    While scholars scoff at building paradise;
For those who fetch and carry for their neighbours,
    Or wash the sick or sit beside the frail,
For those who earn a pittance for their labours,
    But never play the martyred tattletale:

For those for whom a word of thanks suffices,
    Or deem that it was meant, if never said,
For those who run a mile from fame's devices,
    And hide their medals underneath the bed;
For those who slave in worn out wards and clinics,
    Or work beside the nurses, hand in glove,
For those who pay no mind to whining cynics,
    Who know the worth, if not the price, of love:

For those who give their lives to teaching others,
    Yet never learn the meaning of conceit,
For those who treat the homeless as their brothers,
    For men who empty bins and sweep the street;
For volunteers who listen — but don't lecture,
    For coppers who would rather wear no gun,
For juries who can cast aside conjecture
    And steel themselves to do what must be done:

For friends who keep their temper, yet stay candid,
    For citizens who stand up to the yobs,
For those who bring up children single-handed,
    For companies who tailor-make them jobs;
For those who blew the whistle as they hung us,
    For those who stood when you and I would fall,
For these, the unsung heroes here among us:
    Please raise your glass to bless them, one and all.

[DORSINGTON]

[182]

Time Future's Arc

Time Future's arc, dear heart, is long,
 Far, far too long to search its slopes
For silent larks at evensong,
 Or charlatans with horoscopes
 And hollow hopes —

Those pensioned fools who plod and plough
 To gild the rot of golden years,
Who spurn the joys of here and now,
 Their blindfolds wet from bartered tears
 And martyr's fears.

You'll meet them soon enough, dear heart.
 They'll ask you what you want to be
When you 'grow up'. Tell them the cart
 Of life is pulled by mystery —
 Not history!

And when they cluck in mild alarm
 Smile sweetly, dear, as you advance,
And murmur while you trace their palm:
 'Time Future we must leave to chance —
 Come, let us dance!'

[MUSTIQUE]

Dark Matter

'What is matter?'
 '*Never mind.*'
  'What is mind?'
  'No *matter.*'

'What's the Big Bang?'
 '*Dust aligned.*'
  'Dust that went
  a-scatter?'

'*Scattered, aye, in
 galaxies.*'
  'What of the
  Creator?

'Is He just a
 fallacy?
  Is God dead?'
  'No *data!*'

'Why do stars flee?'
 '*No-one knows.*'
  'Are black holes
  a bubble?'

'The universe just
grows and grows.
Read your Planck
and Hubble!'

'Has it got
no boundary?'
'No less than
your chatter.'

'What's dark matter?'
'Pardon me?'
'Never mind.'
'No matter!'

[DORSINGTON]

"The universe has no boundary. (The use of the singular is deliberate.)" Prof. Stephen Hawking, choosing the words to appear on a representation of his laptop computer for a bronze statue of himself commissioned by the author and created by Steven Gregory in 1999.

'I looked at a rook...'

I looked at a rook,
He looked at me,
I in my nook,
He in his tree.

He gave such a look
Of scorn and pride,
I shut my book
And crept inside;

I took from a hook
My gun to kill
That haughty rook,
Who meant me ill;

But just as I took
Most careful aim
He gave me a look
That said: *'For shame!*

Before ye came, long, long ago,
These woods were haunt of rook and crow,
Of badger and wolf and doe in flight —
A squirrel could swing from Dale to Bight —
Ye think me rude to thus intrude
Upon thy paltry solitude?
And yet thy gun much ruder is,
For which of us intruder is?'

I looked at the rook,
He looked at me,
I in my nook,
He in his tree;

Back to its hook
Went gun — and, aye,
Back to my nook
Went book and I.

[CANDLEWOOD]

'Where knowledge falters...'

Where knowledge falters, there men's minds may roam
Upon the shipwrecked shores of outcast thought,
To toy with dreams amid an alien foam,
Conceiving madness doctrine would abort.
A single footprint haunted Darwin's hopes;
I know he spied it — cursed it; feared its tread
Would draw him from the Mount of Olive's slopes
To his disgrace. And where Lucretius led
He followed, step by step; to forge a path,
Beyond the pale, beyond all 'wild surmise',
Through monstrous landscapes, risking bishop's wrath,
His heresy the victim of his eyes.
    When knowledge falters, men must weigh the odds —
    To seek the finch's beak — or serve their gods.

[MUSTIQUE]

"The limit of man's knowledge on any subject possesses a high interest, which is perhaps increased by its close neighbourhood to the realms of the imagination." — Charles Darwin *Journal of Researches into the Geology and Natural History of the Various Countries Visited by HMS Beagle* (1839)

"For it is not true as I think, that the race of mortal creatures were let down from on high by some golden chain..." — Titus Lucretius Carus *De Rerum Natura* [On the Nature of Things] [*1st century BC*]

It is commonly believed that unaccountable differences in the shapes of the beaks of finches in the Galapagos Islands were responsible for first alerting Darwin to the need for a theory of evolution. Charles Darwin is a great hero of mine, and yet Titus Lucretius, an adherent to the philosophy of Epicurus, walked those heretical shores long before him, anticipating both evolution, atomic theory and the concept of entropy by more than two thousand years.

Pitch and Toss

For thirty years at pitch and toss
    in Mammon's inky halls,
I hurled benighted dice across
    the stone of hazard's walls,
      and little reckoned win or loss.
The game was all; the rest was dross.

As living ghosts, a world apart,
    we toiled in lucre's maze,
The sun shut out of each man's heart,
    the glittering lamps ablaze;
      we little reckoned stop from start,
The Midas touch was all our art.

In frenzied play, at fever pitch,
    we sought to build our store,
While Lady Luck, a slattern bitch,
    would taunt us from the door;
      we little reckoned who was which:
The newly poor, the filthy rich.

And there I built my dragon hoard
    of silver and of gold,
And bound it with a miser's cord
    to gnaw when I grew old,
      and little reckoned fire or sword,
And thought myself a mighty lord.

'Til falling sick at last, I stepped
    to seek the open sky,
To bribe the guards with all I'd kept
    to lead me out to die.
      I little reckoned as I wept
That joy into my soul had crept.

But joy in want — is joy deferred,
    and paupers' lives are short,
Fresh worms are for the early bird
    and I was good for nought;
      a fool might reckon what occurred:
They took me back without a word.

[MUSTIQUE]

The Taking of Saddam
[A Ballad]

"Have you ever seen a prudent, calculating dictator? They all become mad." — Benito Mussolini in 1945 from 'Mussolini: A New Life' by Nicholas Farrell, Weidenfeld & Nicolson (2003)

He dared not wear his homburg hat
   For fear of traitors' eyes;
His mind was full of traitors' names,
   His mouth was full of sighs;
He stroked a beard he longed to shave,
   And scanned disloyal skies.

From night to night, from bed to bed,
   The vermin at his heels,
He stumbled through a faithless land
   With faithless imbeciles:
To snatch at sleep— to learn to dread
   The squeal of armoured wheels;

To run, to hide, to live amongst
   The stench of lesser men,
To bribe the tribes he'd fattened once
   Like bullocks in a pen.
His sons both dead so rumour said:
   But who knew how or when?

He glanced about the compound walls,
   The taxi parked nearby,
He smelled the river to the West
   And listened to the sky,
A sky of blades and Black Hawk raids:
   He had no wish to die.

These foreign fools were feeble lords,
　They lived from vote to vote,
He'd but to prime his bombs and wait,
　To stake the tethered goat,
To bide his time and flush them out,
　To seize them by the throat.

They raved of 'freedom', meaning oil,
　The freedom to make war
With weapons they denied to those
　They cast beyond the law;
Denied to all— except the crumbs
　They fed their Jewish whore.

What laws were these but silken hoods
　To blind Saladin's gleam,
To slay with Stealth and stolen wealth,
　To crush the Arab dream,
To bring a people to their knees
　For jackals to redeem?

*　*　*

When tyrants ride the tiger's back
　Their tigers must be fed,
On what and where they little care
　If but the meat be red;
Nor ever do they dare dismount,
　Or stop to count the dead.

His tigers now cried out for meat,
　And meat he must provide.
Invaders' flesh is sweet and fresh,
　Made sweeter by their pride,
The land would rise, a million eyes
　Would leave no place to hide.

No matter that they loved him not,
   That traitors spat and hissed,
His people loved the Yankee less,
   His people would resist!
He pulled some papers from a case
   And ticked names off a list.

If, like all men, they feared to die,
   Their masters feared far more
Those coffin flags and 'body bags'
   Now mounting by the score;
They feared the one-eyed alchemist,
   The First Amendment's roar!

The roar of mice in tailored suits
   On 'CBS Tonight',
The viewer polls and Barbie Dolls
   The satellites of trite,
The endless drone of talking heads
   Who bark but never bite.

Crusaders come — crusaders go,
   They know no history,
Their tents are filled with broken gifts,
   Of miracles to be
From lands sunk in the arid sands
   Of slack democracy.

These padded fools who strode a land
   Where Sargon wrote the law,
Would feel the lash of ancient winds,
   A land in love with war;
A land of death and Allah's breath,
   A land of guile and gore.

Their fathers were all painted apes
    When Ishtar birthed a son,
A son whose deeds begat the seeds
    Of all that men had done,
Whose towers rose long centuries
    Before the Celt or Hun.

He knew himself a lesser man,
    A man of whips and fear,
Unloved, unloving, forged in hate,
    Whose time was drawing near;
Yet each man dies, and this he knew —
    That pain is but veneer.

The-Land-Between-The-Rivers' oil
    Would flow, his will, or no;
If men would ride the tiger's back,
    They reap what tigers sow,
The scripted roars and fake applause
    Were but the tools of show.

But deaths! the deaths of Yankee sons,
    Would echo from the sky!
Fresh coffin flags and 'body bags'
    To feed a camera's eye—
And in a land where mothers vote
    The price might rise too high.

When tyrants ride the tiger's back
    Their tigers must be fed,
On what and where they little care
    If but the meat be red:
Another's life had taught him this:
    And Stalin died in bed.

                        * * *

[194]

His thoughts slid back to glory days
  When all the world was young,
When he had raised his people high
  And slit the Persian tongue,
When enemies went on their knees —
  The same who wished him hung!

Across the river, gleaming white,
  A marble hymn of praise
Stood empty by the Tigris bank,
  Half-hidden in the haze,
A palace for the Ace of Spades,
  To mock his tiger's gaze,

He did not miss the cushioned rooms,
  The onyx baths and showers,
The fountains glittering in the sun,
  The vases full of flowers,
The empty lives of pampered wives —
  He missed his stolen powers:

The right to give, the right to take,
  The drug all leaders crave,
To bid, to send, to crush, to rend,
  To raise up, or enslave;
By Allah's will he'd grasp it still
  Or seek a martyr's grave.

He heard the shouts of startled men,
  The roaring of a beast,
The rumbling breath of whirling death,
  A dragon come to feast,
He lurched across the littered ground
  And stared towards the East.

The enemy! With practised steps
　　He dropped without a sound,
Feet first down through a concrete hole
　　He screwed his body round,
He heard them drop the plastic top,
　　And sank upon the ground.

Some men are born of patient mind
　　To curb a savage wit,
Though tyrants ride the tiger's back,
　　Yet biters may be bit
If one but waits to storm the gates
　　And cast them in the pit!

He waited now — no way to know
　　If worst had come to worst;
A tiger in a spider's hole,
　　His throat was dry with thirst;
He snapped the light, retrieved his gun,
　　Then bit his nails and cursed.

＊ ＊ ＊

Four lines from Hafiz haunted him–
　　A dying tiger lay
Beside a wounded hawk, who sang,
　　'All slayers live to slay,
As we have lived so shall we die,
　　The hunter now is prey.'

A roar of trucks, the stamp of boots,
　　He killed the neon light,
The darkness swooped around him then,
　　A darkness more than night;
A choice to make, but which to take:
　　Negotiate, or fight?

He whispered out the English words,
   'I am the Pres-i-dent...'
A sudden shout — much louder now,
   'A vent! I've found a vent!'
'As we have lived so shall we die...'
   The dogs were on the scent!

The gun lay cold beneath his hand,
   His hand lay by his hip,
A deadly thing — a hawk to sing!
   His fingers stroked the grip;
He twisted up his hand to bring
   Its muzzle to his lip.

When tyrants ride the tigers back,
   The tigers must be fed,
He thought of myth, of kin and kith,
   Of rulers in his stead,
A simple choice: a martyr's voice!
   But who reveres the dead?

He tapped the barrel on his teeth,
   Its oil upon his tongue;
A gentle squeeze would end it now,
   Far quicker than be hung;
He heard the wing beats of a hawk,
   A hawk that had not sung!

The dead do not write history,
   The dead can only rot,
While victors reinvent the past
   Of what, and what was not.
He made an arc, and in the dark
   The gun dropped by his cot.

He would not die here in this hole,
    He must 'ne-go-shee-ate',
He whispered out the word again,
    He had not long to wait,
He heard the squeal of styrofoam,
    The jackals at the gate!

His tiger made one ghostly leap,
    And now, he stood alone—
When tyrants ride the tiger's back,
    Their madness is their own.
A wary shout, his arms reached out
    To scrabble on the stone.

He had not worn his homburg hat
    For fear of traitors' eyes;
His mind was full of shameful lies,
    His mouth was full of sighs,
He stood and spoke eleven words
    Beneath disloyal skies.

[MUSTIQUE]

Saddam Hussein was captured on December 13, 2003. He was found hidden in a 'spider hole' about six feet underground in the courtyard of a farmhouse outside the city of Tikrit. He had a pistol, but did not attempt to use it. His first words to US forces were: 'I am the President of Iraq and I wish to negotiate.'

Wishes

Wishes are posies that wither and fade
In chapels of ease full of flowers and verse,
Where the beds are as wide as a sexton's spade,
And the roofs as snug as a landlord's purse.

Wishes are fishes that swim in the nets
Of castaways souls by the shores of the dead,
Where coins are as rare as a ferryman's debts,
And nobody cares what you did or you said.

Wishes come skipping and eager to play
In the ravenous dreams of childless wives;
Wishes are thoroughbreds feasting on hay
While beggars must walk for all of their lives.

Wishes are nooses to collar the rich
And throttle the rest of us stood in the queue;
I'll make you a wish, you sonofabitch:
May all of your wishes, but one, come true!

[DORSINGTON]

Falling, falling
[September 11, 2001]

Mommy! Mommy! Come and see!
The lady says it's history
Falling on 'hew-man-ity'.
Mommy! Mommy! Come and see!

All the world is calling, calling;
All the world is falling, falling...

Mommy! Mommy! Please don't cry.
Things are falling from the sky,
Look! A man has learned to fly!
Mommy! Mommy! Please don't cry.

All the world is calling, calling,
All the world is falling, falling...

Mommy, who was that who called?
See where all the smoke has crawled!
Mommy! Look! The tower has falled!
Mommy, who was that who called?

All the world is calling, calling;
All the world is falling,
        f
       a
       l
       l
        i
        n
        g

Index

Performer and song titles for 'Lines', page 78

1   The Who / 'My Generation'
2   Chuck Berry / 'Memphis, Tennessee'
3   Harry Belanfonte / 'Island In The Sun'
4   Bobby Fuller Four / 'I Fought The Law (And The Law Won)'
5   Robert Johnson / 'Me And The Devil Blues'
6   The Zombies / 'She's Not There'
7   The Rolling Stones / 'Paint It Black'
8   Ray Charles / 'Hit The Road, Jack'
9   The Doors / 'Light My Fire'
10   Leonard Cohen / 'Bird On A Wire'
11   Buddy Holly / 'Maybe Baby'
12   Bob Dylan / 'It's All Over Now, Baby Blue'
13   Elvis Presley / 'Heartbreak Hotel'
14   Sam Cooke / 'Wonderful World'
15   The Beatles / 'Please Please Me'
16   Gene Chandler / 'Duke Of Earl'
17   Memphis Slim / 'Mortgage on My Love'
18   The Isley Brothers / 'Twist And Shout'
19   Chris Montez / 'Let's Dance'
20   Van Morrison / 'Moondance'
21   Bob Dylan / 'Just Like A Woman'
22   Janis Joplin / 'Oh Lord, Won't You Buy Me A Mercedes-Benz'
23   Elvis Presley / 'Love Me Tender'
24   Creedence Clearwater Revival / 'Willy And The Poor Boys'
25   Lou Reed / 'Walk On The Wild Side'
36   Little Richard / 'Tutti Frutti'

Acknowledgements

PERMISSION FROM *Tree News* to reprint Bill Sanderson's illustration for 'Go not to the walnut tree' is gratefully acknowledged.

I have tested the patience and affection of close friends and colleagues, using them as guinea-pigs while reciting my poetry hot-off-the-laser-writer. Let me thank them all here unreservedly — especially Dick Pountain, Marion Hills, Don Atyeo, Sue Ready, Eric Shaw, Bud & Patsy Fisher, Robin Miller, Mick Farren, John and Maggie Lagana, Brian and Johanna Alexander, Peter and Barbara Godfrey, Bob and Beverly Bartner, Susan and Ian Leggett, Robin and Rachelle Kent, George and Catherine Snow and the entire Mannings family.

I owe heartfelt thanks to my editor, Simon Rae. There is not a 'thee', a 'thine', or a 'thou' in *Lone Wolf* that he has not attempted to excise!

Moni Mannings somehow finds time from her legal practise to read every poem I write. Not to vet them legally, of course, but to comment from a very different perspective from my own — that of a wife, a mother and an 'ordinary' person. I am very grateful for her enthusiasm and gentle mockery. She is no 'ordinary' person.

My thanks to George Taylor, Lou and Dan for their patience and technical wizardry on the spoken-word CD. And to Mike Dunn for his first class book design and Bill Sanderson, as ever, for his superb illustrations.

Michael Boyd and Fiona Lindsay from the Royal Shakespeare Company could not have been kinder as they persuaded me that I *could* stand in front of a huge audience reading my verse, surrounded by some of the best stage actors in the world, and not make a complete hash of it. They were right, too, that the RSC would pack the Swan Theatre for 'Did I Mention the Free Wine?'

Sue Freestone and James Nightingale at Hutchinson continue to offer unfailing support and throw a mean launch party.

My poetry tours are an intrinsic part of my life now. Bruce Sawford and Steve Kotok headed up the tours in the UK and US respectively like the old pros they are. Mick, Tom and Mark from Class Act humped and trucked and lit and sound-checked from Monterey to Glasgow. Patrick 'Why-can't-we-ever-get-a-decent-hotel?' Song did magic work on the giant projection screen.

Ian Leggett and Catherine Bishop handled the finances. This is not a job for the faint-hearted. Alistair Ramsay and Stephen Colvin, CEO's of Dennis Publishing in the UK and the USA respectively, have put up cheerfully with their Chairman's tyrannical appropriation of designers, marketing and internet gurus and other personnel. I thank them and all the staff at Dennis Publishing.

Of course, nothing (in Britain or America) can be done without lawyers. My thanks, then, to Simons, Muirhead & Burton in London and Jacobs, DeBrauwere & Dehn in New York City.

Sarah Braben of The Braben Company in Britain and Drew Kerr and his team at Four Corners in New York have led me around (and, when I insisted, *into*) the minefield of media relations for many years. With me as a client they all deserve medals.

The unflappable Caroline Rush and Alex Patrick oversaw the production of *Lone Wolf*, and brought it in on budget and on time. I am indebted to them both.

Guy Sneesby at Dennis Interactive worked with his talented team of internet designers and editors to produce a wonderful website for me at **www.felixdennis.com**. Do check it out next time you are surfing the internet.

An Australian film-maker, Fiona Prendergast, followed me around for weeks shooting a film of the tour called 'Did I Mention the Free Wine?' — and I only lost my temper once! The film is a knockout. (Early first editions of this book will hopefully contain a free DVD of 'Did I Mention the Free Wine?' If your book does not, then go to **www.felixdennis.com** to view clips.)

My personal staff, Wendy Kasabian, David Bliss, Amy Tranter, Michael Hyman, Lloyd Warren, Cathy Galt, Toby Fisher and Sharon Islam have done everything from tucking their boss up in bed to piloting helicopters. Er, actually it was Castle Air who flew the helicopters and Key Air who provided the jet planes and crew.

Everything I write is composed on one of eight Apple Macintosh computers around the world. Touch wood, not one of them has ever let me down, thanks to expert IT maintenance from Fiona Pye's team and Volchok Consulting. Underneath the desk of one of those computers there usually lay a small orange ball of fur, hogging the air-conditioning. Her name was Licky— a bitch I inherited from David Bowie when I bought his house in Mustique. Licky heard many of these poems first, and although she never understood a word of them, her presence was a constant comfort. Sadly, she died a few months ago.

The love of my life, Marie-France Demolis, goes on cheering from the wings, a glass of Burgundy in hand, along with Suzen Murakoshi and Lisa Chong Rim Patnode. My left-shoulder daemon continues to misbehave himself, (waking me at inappropriate hours of the night with new lines of verse), while the shade of my old friend Michael Nixon still urges me on to seek for 'What Lies Hidden'.